A PIONEER STORY

THE DAILY LIFE OF A
CANADIAN FAMILY IN 1840

Kids Can Press acknowledges the financial support of the Ontario Arts
Council, the Canada Council for the Arts and the Government of
Canada, through the BPIDP, for our publishing activity.

Published in Canada by
Kids Can Press Ltd.
29 Birch Avenue
Toronto, ON M4V 1E2

www.kidscanpress.com

Edited by Valerie Wyatt
Designed by Blair Kerrigan / Glyphics
Printed and bound in Canada

CDN 94 0 9 8 7 6 5 4 3 2 1
CDN PA 94 0 9

National Library of Canada Cataloguing in Publication Data

Greenwood, Barbara, [date.]
        A pioneer story : the daily life of a Canadian family in 1840

Includes index.
ISBN 978-1-55074-237-4 (bound)   ISBN 978-1-55074-128-5 (pbk.)

1. Frontier and pioneer life — Canada — Juvenile literature.   2. Canada
— Social life and customs — 19th century — Juvenile literature.* 3.
Frontier and pioneer life — Canada — Juvenile fiction.   I. Collins,
Heather.   II. Title.

FC88.G74 1994   j971.04   C94-931093-X
F1021.G74 1994

Kids Can Press is a *lorus*™ Entertainment company

A PIONEER STORY

THE DAILY LIFE OF A
CANADIAN FAMILY IN 1840

WRITTEN BY BARBARA GREENWOOD
ILLUSTRATED BY HEATHER COLLINS

KIDS CAN PRESS

Acknowledgements

My thanks go first to Catherine Parr Traill, Susanna Moodie, Mary O'Brien and the many other settlers who not only "roughed it in the bush" but who left detailed and spirited accounts of their experiences.

I would also like to thank Rosemary Kovacs of Black Creek Pioneer Village for helping me experience the sounds and smells of pioneer life; my editor, Valerie Wyatt, whose ability to focus on the main point was an invaluable help in shaping the material; Heather Collins, who created such endearing faces for my characters; and, as always, my husband, Robert E. Greenwood, for ferreting out arcane details, engineering several of the activities and providing the leaven of laughter.

BG

I would like to thank the people at Kids Can Press, who were totally supportive through all the highs and lows of the longest book I've ever illustrated. And thanks especially to Barbara, for a wonderful story, the stacks of visual research, and for always having the answer to my questions. Her help made illustrating the hundreds of details of 1840s life a pleasure.

Also, thank you to my models, who made the Robertson family come alive — Sally Palmateer and her children, Norah and Graham, and Declan Whelehan and his daughter, Sinead. And, as always, thank you to my family: Blair for his support and patience, Brooke for her humour, and Max, who never minded donning a shawl or a loincloth.

HC

To Bernice, Jean, Kathi, Pat, Sonja and Vancy — valued friends and writing-workshop colleagues
BG

For my mother and father
HC

CONTENTS

THE ROBERTSONS

Meet the Robertsons, a pioneer family living on a backwoods farm in eastern Canada in 1840. Although the Robertsons are a made-up family, their struggle to clear the forest, to plant, to harvest and to make a good life for themselves echoes the efforts of our early settlers, who worked hard to build a home, a community and a country.

The Robertsons, like real-life settlers, live by this motto:

Eat it up,
Wear it out,
Make it do,
Or go without.

The Robertson children learn early that "many hands make light work" and that it's best to "make hay while the sun shines." But life isn't all chores and making do. Maple-sugar frolics and harvest suppers, husking bees and barn dances, the birth of lambs and the search for a honey tree brighten the days as the seasons pass from winter to spring, from summer to fall.

Lizzie   Meg and Tommy   George

Pa Robertson   Ma Robertson   Sarah   Granny   Willy

SIGNS OF SPRING

Sarah wiggled away from the cold strip at the edge of the straw mattress. She tugged gently at the quilt, trying not to disturb her older sister. Meg would be annoyed if she woke up. It's her own fault, grumbled Sarah to herself. Thinks she can hog the covers just because she's bigger. Again she gave a tiny tug and managed to ease a hand's-width of quilt to her side of the bed. Between Sarah and Meg, four-year-old Lizzie flopped over, then curled again into a tight ball.

A tickling sensation told Sarah she'd soon have to use the cold potty hidden under the bed. But not just yet. She curled closer to Lizzie, trying to keep warm, wishing she could drift back into her dream. She'd been running barefoot up the hill where the new house would be built. The sun was hot, a warm breeze blew through her hair … If only the warm weather would come. It had been winter for so long.

Early-morning sounds chased away the last bit of sleepiness — a bubbly snore as Granny started to wake in the bed across the room, the scratchings of a poker stirring the fire to life in the outer room, the soft whump of the door as her father went out to feed the animals, the creak of the ladder as one of her brothers climbed down from the loft.

But there was another sound — a small, steady tap, tap. What could it be? Where was it? Outside? She stared at the closed wooden shutters through which seeped cold, grey light. Tap, tap, tap, tap. On and on. Water dripping, she thought. The snow on the roof is melting. Her heart gave a bound. Snow's melting! It's spring. It's spring!

Ignoring the icy floor, Sarah scrambled into her clothes.

"Dress me, Sary." Lizzie yawned, sitting up in her warm nest.

"Ask Meg." Sarah skipped out of the room before Lizzie could start to whine. "Did you hear it, Ma?"

"Hear what, hinny?" Her mother was standing at the table, pounding down bread dough. "Just give Tommy a wee walk about, there's a good lass. He's grizzling for his breakfast."

Sarah lifted her baby brother from the cradle and jiggled him up and down. Soon he was sucking contentedly on his thumb. "Listen!" she said. "It's louder now. Don't you hear it?"

Her mother stopped and cocked her head to one side. From outside came a steady, splashy plop, plop, plop. A smile lit her face. "Spring," she said. "Spring at last."

By the time Pa and George and Willy were back in from feeding the animals, everyone else was up and dressed and ready for breakfast.

"Snow's melting," Pa announced, spooning up his oatmeal. Over breakfast they chattered and laughed, making plans for the spring work. After a winter of huddling by the fire, everyone wanted to be out and doing.

Halfway through the morning, with the noontime stew bubbling over the fire, Ma said, "Sarah, run away out and clear a place for the hens."

"But there's still snow on the ground."

"Not for long. And it's time those hens were out and about if we're ever to have eggs again. Take a handful of the crushed corn and some bran to spread for them."

Sarah pinned a heavy blanket shawl around her head and shoulders and pulled on the mitts she had knitted herself that winter. Her moccasined feet were padded with thick socks, but even so, she felt the cold of wet snow through them. Soft, dry snow was much warmer to walk in, but still, it was good to see the snow melting.

As she trudged out to the barn, carrying the bowl of feed and a twig broom, she looked for other signs of spring. On the sunny side of each building the snow had begun to shrink away, showing patches of brown earth. Soon, green shoots would push through the snow. Last spring, she'd brought the first dandelion leaves home. Her mouth watered at the thought of fresh greens for supper. How soon could she go hunting for them this year?

The hen house was a small box snuggled up to the barn. "Here's a warm day for you, my dearies," Sarah called, imitating Granny's Scottish accent. Granny was good with hens. "Come along out." The rooster was first down the ramp when she opened the little door. He strutted importantly, waiting for her to sweep the snow away from the sheltered spot in front of the hen house.

As she scattered the feed, first one sharp beak and then two poked inquisitively out of the low doorway. Soon, all four hens were clucking and scratching and pecking on the patch of cleared earth. "You work nice and hard," Sarah encouraged them, just the way Granny always did. How

wonderful it would be to have fresh eggs. She hadn't had a taste of one since last November.

A big brown hen, Granny's favourite, was having trouble keeping her mind on eating. She ran about in a dither, clucking and flapping.

"What's wrong with you, then?" Sarah asked, shooing the hen back to the corn. "You scratch away there." But the hen kept making little darts at the door, then changing her mind. "You look all broody," Sarah said. Suddenly she remembered what Granny had said about broody hens.

What if … Sarah turned the wooden peg and opened the big door of the hen house. Slatted nesting boxes sat on the shelf. Sarah took off her mitten and ran her fingers through the straw in each box. Nothing. For a moment she'd allowed herself to hope. "I guess Ma's right. It *is* too early for eggs."

She closed the door. The hens had scattered. Two of them were around the corner in front of the barn. "Stay in the sun," Sarah urged, shooing them with her broom. But the big brown hen ducked away and ran at the open barn door. On mild winter days, the hens had been given the run of the barn for a few hours before being shut up in their own quarters. As the hen dashed through the door, Sarah had a sudden thought. "Watch those hens now," Granny was always saying. "They'll hide their eggs on you, sure as scat."

Sarah stood in the gloom of the barn and watched the hen pick away at ends of grain hanging over the mow. Then, with a sudden dart, the hen was gone. "Got you," Sarah said, diving after her. She reached an arm far into the hay until she felt the soft warmth of feathers. Ignoring the agitated pecking, Sarah felt under the hen until her hand found what she was seeking. Gently she drew it out — a perfect white egg. She could hardly believe her eyes. Cradling it in two hands, she walked carefully back to the cabin.

"*There* you are," Ma said as she opened the door. "Just bang the pot for the men. We're ready to eat."

"Look!" Sarah held the egg out and, with a surprised intake of breath, they all crowded around.

Ma stroked the egg dreamily. "Pudding," she said. "I'll make a nice egg pudding for tonight's supper. There'll be a good mouthful for each of us."

INSIDE THE LOG HOUSE

Work must have seemed never-ending to the early settlers. Every pair of hands was needed to keep the family fed and clothed. Inside the house the women prepared the big meal of the day, which was eaten at noon.

Next year, Lizzie (4 years old) will start doing simple chores such as setting the table or helping to dry the dishes.

Sarah (10 years old) helps wind the yarn. She also gives the cradle a rock whenever baby Tommy cries.

Granny spins sheep's wool into yarn on the spinning wheel she brought with her from Scotland.

Mrs. Robertson lifts a loaf of bread out of the bake kettle. Early that morning she had put the dough (which had risen overnight) into the kettle and settled it among the coals to bake.

Meg (15 years old) mixes flour and water to make dumplings. She will drop the dumplings into the stew bubbling over the fire.

George (13 years old) and Willy (9 years old) sleep in the loft on straw ticks laid directly on the floor.

A small storeroom holds two barrels of salted pork, a basket of potatoes (covered to keep them from freezing), a barrel of salt and pots and pans not needed for today's meal.

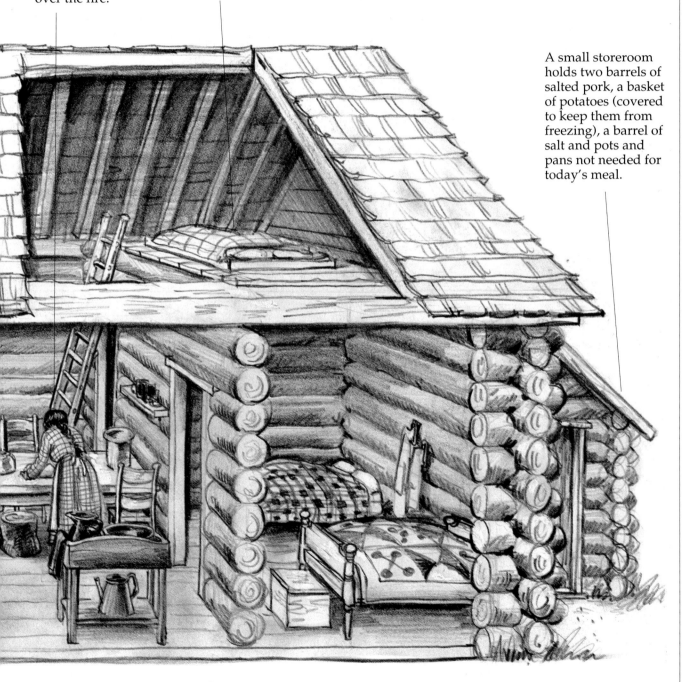

COOKING

Cooking over an open fire was dangerous. The cook could be burned or scalded as she leaned near the fire. Often she had to beat out sparks that landed on her skirt. Women and children wore heavy wool winter and summer because it didn't catch fire as easily as cotton.

To make the pots easier to reach, the fireplace was fitted with an iron "crane." The long arm could swing over the fire or out into the room. Kettles and pots were hung from this arm on hooks. Hooks of different lengths controlled how near to the fire the pot hung.

Pans and flat-bottomed kettles were often set right in the fire. One type of pan, fitted with long legs, was called a spider. Meat was often hung on a string above the fire. It had to be turned constantly so it would roast evenly. Some cooks were lucky enough to have a clock jack with a strong spring that turned the meat mechanically.

The food was plain and often tasteless. For most of the year the family lived on boiled potatoes, fried pork, stews and soups. Dried herbs improved the taste a little. Vegetables were added to the pot in summer and for as long as they lasted in winter. By March the vegetables might be used up or mouldy, and the settlers might have only porridge left to eat. As soon as the snow disappeared, the children searched the woods for greens such as wild leeks and cow cabbage.

FEAR OF FIRE

Y ou watch out for that fire, lassie," Granny warned as Sarah jumped back, beating at the sparks on her skirt. "'Tis a good servant, is fire, but a bad master."

Sarah sighed and picked at the little scorch hole. She'd have to mend it. She'd been so careful all winter to keep her new dress free from burns. Why couldn't the stupid spark have landed on her apron?

Scorch holes were the price everyone paid for working close to an open fire. Sparks showered out of the fireplace. Pots tipped, emptying out scalding liquid. Fat, dripping from meat, caught fire. Sleeves or aprons burst into flames. To fight sudden fires, every household kept a bucket or two of water by the fireplace. If embers tumbled out onto the hearth, they were swept back into the fire with a goose wing kept handy on the mantelpiece.

Chimneys were also dangerous. Soot coating the inside of the chimney often caught fire, sending sparks showering over the wooden roof. Many households had a ladder permanently fastened to the roof so that someone could climb up quickly with a bucket of water. If a fire started, the family tried to smother it with wet quilts. Sometimes it was too late. Then the only thing to do was drag as much as possible from the cabin and watch while years of work went up in smoke.

Prevention was the better way. To have water on hand, settlers built as close to a stream or a spring as possible. They cleaned out their chimneys at least twice a year. It was a dirty job, pushing a broom down the chimney. Soot billowed into the room, covering everything, getting up noses and down throats. But the mess and discomfort were better than a fire. To keep the chimney as clean as possible, early settlers burned hard wood rather than soft wood such as pine, which left a sticky, inflammable gum on the inside of the chimney. But in spite of the precautions, each year someone in the neighbourhood would be burned out.

When iron stoves became available, families could hardly wait to get one. Imagine being able to trap that fire in an iron box where it cooked and heated for you but didn't jump out to burn you — a good servant, kept in place, mastered at last.

THE FARMYARD

The barn is used for storing grain and hay or grass for the animals. There is a small stable for the family's oxen and milk cows. Behind the barn, on the warm, south side, is a shelter for sheep.

Stones cleared from the fields will be used to make the cellar walls of the new house.

The bake oven is used in good weather. In winter, Mrs. Robertson bakes indoors in a kettle.

Sarah bangs on a pot with a spoon to call everyone in for the noon meal.

Mr. Robertson will haul the logs he has cut to the sawmill, where they will be sawn into boards for the Robertsons' new house.

This shanty was the very first shelter the family built. Now it is used as a workshop. Almost everything on a backwoods farm has to be made by hand: furniture, sleds, cupboards, animal pens.

A pail of lye is kept in the privy. Once a day a cupful is thrown down the hole to keep the odour tolerable. Pieces of dried corncobs are used as toilet paper.

Willy and George haul water for the family and the animals. Next they will split wood for the fire.

MAPLE SUGARING

We *won't* be in the way," Sarah insisted. "We'll be good helpers. Won't we, Willy?"

"Remember how we dragged all those stones out of the field last summer?" Willy pointed out. "A bucket full of sap wouldn't be any heavier than rocks."

They were trudging after their mother along the snowy path to the wood lot.

"All right." Ma sighed. "We could use the help. Why do things have to happen when we're so busy?" She hunched her shawl around her shoulders. "But you have to do exactly what you're told. We don't want any more accidents."

Sarah's stomach flipped as she remembered her father hobbling into the house, blood oozing through the scarf he'd knotted around his leg. "Axe slipped," he'd grunted, collapsing on a chair.

The sugarbush was far back in the wood lot. Sarah's fingers and nose felt like icicles by the time the sweet tang of maple syrup drifted through the trees.

Willy licked his lips. "I can hardly wait," he said.

"Don't you try sneaking any," his mother warned. "I don't want you burnt. You'll get some later, when we're done."

"Yes, Ma." Willy rolled his eyes at Sarah.

In the clearing three black kettles hung over three fires. Meg was leaning over one, both hands clutching a paddle as she stirred. "I'm so tired," she burst out, the minute she saw them. "I think this batch is ready. I didn't know how I was going to pour it alone." She gave a big sniff and drew her hand under her nose.

Sarah stared at her older sister. Was Meg going to cry?

"It's all right, Meg. Let me have a look." Ma took the stirring paddle, lifted some of the brown syrup and let it run back into the pot. "Yes, it looks ready. Has George brought some fresh sap?"

"A bit." Meg nodded towards a barrel standing nearby in the snow.

As Ma ladled the fresh sap into an empty kettle, Sarah looked around. She hadn't helped with the sugaring before. She'd only been out for the final evening, when they scraped the last of the sticky syrup out of the pot and drizzled it on the snow to make candy.

"How's Pa?" Meg asked.

"He'll be fine. We got the leg bound up and the bleeding stopped."

Just then George appeared from the far pathway, the sled rope looped around his chest. He was straining to pull the load into the clearing.

"We'll help." Sarah and Willy jumped up from the log they'd been sitting on.

"Half a barrel," George panted. "All I could manage by myself." He slumped onto the log as Sarah and Willy tugged the sled closer to the fire.

Ma began ladling sap from the barrel on the sled into a kettle. "Was there much more out there?"

"Yup." George rubbed his hands together and stretched his feet out to the fire. "Dozen or so buckets."

"You'll have to fetch it, George. We need it to keep this batch boiling."

"We'll get it." Sarah snatched up the sled rope. "Show us where the sap trees are, George."

George's head jerked up resentfully. Sarah wished she hadn't sounded so bossy. "Please," she added, hoping to wipe the scowl off his face.

"Get a move on, George." Ma sounded impatient.

George glowered at Sarah, then turned to his mother. "Getting dark out there."

"Take some of those pine-knot torches," Ma snapped. "And hurry up about it."

George gathered up the pine knots and lit one. "Come on, then," he growled, and stomped off. Sarah and Willy had learned to be careful of George when he was in a prickly mood. Silently they picked up the sled rope and followed him into the dark forest.

The sled, with its empty barrel, glided easily over the packed snow of the pathway. But soon George plunged into knee-deep snow. The sled lurched and floundered. Even through her wool mitts Sarah could feel the sled rope biting into her palms.

"Wait up, George," Willy called. "We can't pull it through here."

"Thought you wanted to help," his brother jeered. "Just leave it there. You can carry the buckets out to it."

In the gloom Sarah could barely see the dark outlines of buckets standing under the trees.

The first bucket was only a few steps away. Together, Sarah and Willy grabbed the handle and poured the watery sap into the empty barrel on the sled. Sarah's shoulders were aching by the time they'd emptied the next four. She could see by Willy's clenched teeth that he'd never complain, not with George there.

"That's all," Sarah said after they had trudged back and forth a few more times.

"Naw, there's lots more." George hoisted a bucket up and tipped it. "You've only got the close-in trees. Go farther."

"But it's dark." Sarah was dismayed to hear herself. George always sneered at crybabies.

"Take a torch, then."

Sarah looked at Willy, who just shrugged and started off into the trees. "No point arguing with him," he muttered as Sarah, blazing torch in hand, caught up.

They tramped along, scanning the trees. No buckets. No matter what mean old George said, there were no more buckets. Sarah's fingers were freezing. She tucked her free hand into the warmth of her armpit. Then she saw a dark shape just a few steps off the path.

"Here's one, Willy." In the flickering torchlight they could see the bucket on the ground under a dripping spile. Just beyond was the hulk of a fallen tree.

They both reached for the rope handle of the bucket. The torch wavered in Sarah's other hand. She took a firmer grip and suddenly gasped. Beyond the tree shone two yellow eyes. "Willy!" Her mouth was almost too dry to form the words. "Look!"

Low snarling made Sarah's heart pound. In the dim light she saw the tufted ears and heart-shaped face of a lynx.

"Get George," Sarah whispered. The lynx crept towards them. Sarah swung the torch in front of her and the cat backed down the fallen tree. If it ran up high enough to spring on them … "Get George."

Willy started to run. Sarah swung the torch in an arc. The cat hissed and backed off as sparks flew.

The lynx crept closer. Sarah swung the burning brand to face it. Please don't let the torch go out. The cat snarled, skittering sideways. Sarah began to back away. Her shoulders ached from holding her arms stiff and straight. The torch wavered. Please hurry. The cat moved slowly down the sloping trunk. Just keep the fire between us, Sarah told herself, backing away, one step at a time. Then her heel hit something solid. The bucket. She felt her ankle turn, and suddenly she was on the ground. The torch swayed.

"Throw it! Throw it!" George was yelling as he and Willy came crashing along the path.

Sarah raised the torch and flung it with all her might. George ran past her, slinging another torch at the lynx. Then he turned and grabbed her hand, pulling her up and along the path, with Willy running beside them. Through the pounding in her ears Sarah heard the lynx give one long, furious scream, then silence.

Back at the sled, George went from torch to torch, setting them all alight. "Fire," he said in a shaky voice. "They sure hate fire."

He picked up the sled rope, then looked at Sarah. "You all right?"

She nodded. Her heart was still pounding and her ankle twinged, but what did that matter. "Thanks, George. You —"

In the flickering torchlight Sarah thought she saw George's face reddening as he turned away. "Yeah, well …" he interrupted gruffly. "Glad you're safe. Come on. Let's get out of here."

MAKING MAPLE SUGAR

Pioneer families like the Robertsons depended on maple sugar as a sweetener. White sugar, made from West Indian sugar cane, was too expensive for most backwoods families. Even if the family could afford white sugar, someone would have to travel to a town or city to buy it. Instead, the early settlers learned from the Native people how to collect sap from maple trees in the early spring and boil it down to a thick, sweet syrup or a brown sugar.

The first thing to learn was when to collect the sap.

One day in the middle of March, Mr. Robertson decided the days were just mild enough and the nights just frosty enough for the sap to be running. He piled all their buckets onto a sled, and he and George set off for the sugarbush, a small stand of maple trees near the back of their farm.

To collect the sap, they bored a hole in each maple tree, then hammered in a wooden tube called a spile. Under the spile they set a bucket to catch the clear, watery sap.

Each day the buckets of sap were emptied into one large barrel, which was hauled back to the boiling area on a sled. Here, three big iron kettles hung over fires.

To remove twigs, bits of bark and other dirt, the sap was poured through a woollen cloth.

Later, a piece of pork fat was thrown into the boiling sap to clean out smaller particles. The fat made scum rise to the top so it could be skimmed off.

In the first of the three kettles, the watery, tasteless sap was vigorously boiled over a roaring fire. Gradually the water in it evaporated, leaving behind a thicker, sweeter liquid. This was ladled into the second kettle, where it was gently boiled to thicken it more. Constant stirring kept it from burning. This thick, sweet syrup might be poured into jugs to be used on porridge, or it might be ladled into the third kettle. There, over a very small fire, it was carefully stirred until it turned into sugar. The sugar was packed into wooden boxes and tubs to be used in the coming year.

When the sugaring was done, Mrs. Robertson spooned the last of the thick, gooey syrup from the bottom of the kettle and threw it on a patch of clean snow. As the syrup hardened into taffy, everyone broke off bits. What a wonderful treat after the long, hard work of boiling down!

Tapping a Maple Tree

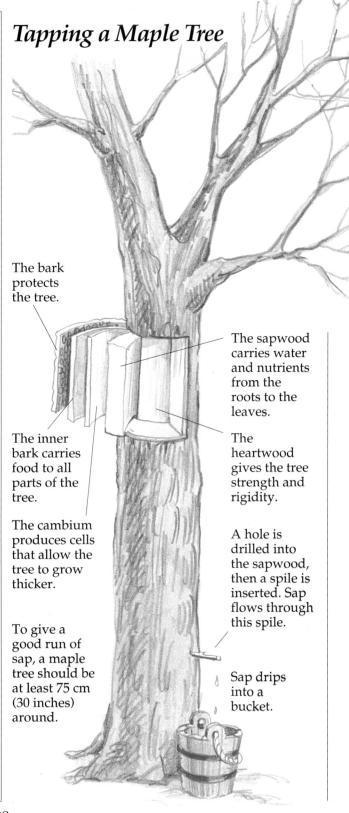

The bark protects the tree.

The inner bark carries food to all parts of the tree.

The cambium produces cells that allow the tree to grow thicker.

To give a good run of sap, a maple tree should be at least 75 cm (30 inches) around.

The sapwood carries water and nutrients from the roots to the leaves.

The heartwood gives the tree strength and rigidity.

A hole is drilled into the sapwood, then a spile is inserted. Sap flows through this spile.

Sap drips into a bucket.

29

EARLY SYRUP MAKING

The Native people, especially the Ojibwa and Iroquois, made maple syrup long before European settlers arrived. During the "sugar moon" or "maple moon," when the weather told them the sap would be running, they gathered in a large stand of maple trees.

To tap a tree, they made a long slash across the trunk with a tomahawk. Into the cut they wedged a flat piece of wood. This directed the dripping sap into a birch-bark bowl on the ground.

When the sap began to flow, they held a thanksgiving ceremony to celebrate the first harvest of the year. Then they began the hard work of making the syrup. Because they had no iron kettles, they may have thickened the syrup by dropping heated rocks into birch-bark containers full of sap.

A Sappy Story

Sap is a watery liquid that carries nutrients from the roots of a tree to its leaves. This happens from early spring until late fall, but only spring sap is sweet enough to make into syrup. Why?

As the cold weather approaches in the late fall, the tree manufactures more sugar than usual. The sugar mixes with the watery sap and acts as an antifreeze to keep the tree from freezing solid in all but the very coldest parts of winter.

In the early spring, when the temperatures are milder, the sap thaws by day even though it may still freeze at night. The alternate freezing and thawing starts the sap flowing. The spring sap stays sweet until the nights are warm and the tree no longer needs its antifreeze.

Try mixing up some sugary antifreeze and see what happens when you freeze it.

You'll need:
- 2 plastic cups
- water
- a spoon
- sugar
- a marker
- a freezer

1. Half fill each cup with water.

2. To one cup, add two heaping spoonfuls of sugar. Stir until the sugar is dissolved. Mark the cup with an S.

3. Place both cups in the freezer. After an hour, compare the contents of the two cups. Which one is frozen? How much longer does it take the other water to freeze?

TORCHES

Back in the days before flashlights, venturing out into the dark night could be scary. To light the way, torches were made from pine wood.

Children were sent into the forest to find fallen pine trees, which were full of a sticky gum-like resin. The logs were chopped into sticks. When lit, the resin made the wood burn brightly and slowly. Sometimes pine knots were used instead. They could be burned on their own, or put in an iron basket called a jack light.

Later, the settlers learned to extract the resin and use it to make longer-burning torches. To do this they started pine chips smouldering, then propped a kettle upside down over the fire. As the black smoke rose it left resin in the kettle. Any stick dipped into the resin could be set alight. Old brooms were often turned into blazing torches.

Torches could be dangerous. Hot resin dripped from them onto hands and clothes. Showers of sparks could set a barn or house on fire. In a dry season, they could start a forest fire. As much as light was needed on a dark night, settlers learned to use their torches sparingly — and with great care.

a jack light

SCHOOL DAYS

"Cry, baby, cry! Cry, baby, cry!"

Willy tried to shield the boy beside him, but he was too late. A snowball smacked wetly against Cecil's ear. Pushing the younger boy around to the side of the school, Willy yelled over his shoulder, "Lay off, Frank O'Flynn!"

"Yeah, yeah. Whatcha gonna do? Tell your big brother?" A second snowball whizzed past.

Willy looked at Cecil, who was blubbering and wiping his nose on his sleeve. Why me? For two whole days, ever since that dreadful moment when Mr. Blount had said, "William Robertson, *you* will take charge of the new boy," Willy had been dodging Frank and his gang.

"Come on," he said, herding Cecil around to the back of the school. "Better to stay away from them." If he was going to be stuck with someone who minced around in town boots and whose drippy nose was always stuck up in the air because it didn't like the smells, the farther he stayed from the big boys the better.

A group of girls had tramped out a big circle in the snow and were chasing one another in a game of fox and geese. Sarah came running over. She looked at Cecil, his face pinched from the cold and puckering again. Then she turned to her brother. "What's wrong with him *this* time?"

"I hate this place!" Cecil burst out. "In England I went to school with gentlemen's sons. And we had a *proper* schoolmaster, not some broken-down old soldier."

Sarah's lips tightened. "Perhaps you should have stayed there," she said curtly. "Wipe your nose, for goodness' sake."

"My father says this neighbourhood is full of louts and layabouts," Cecil muttered as Sarah ran back to the game.

That does it, Willy thought, as he stormed away. Let the snotty little weasel look out for himself.

That afternoon, Mr. Blount announced a spelling bee to practise for the big Saturday-evening contest against the school across the valley. The spelling battle had been raging all winter with turn-about visits between the two schools. Sarah had nearly won the last meet, but in the final round she'd missed out on "Portuguese." It was the third time in a row their school had lost.

"Right! We'll see what we've learned this month." Mr. Blount was rubbing his hands in anticipation as he strode around, lining them up into two teams. "First up, Frank O'Flynn. Spell 'horse.'"

"Horse. H-o-r-s."

"Out! Next."

Willy got the "e" and "i" mixed up in "neighbour." Sarah was going strong until she hit "desiccation." But the marvel of the afternoon was Cecil. No matter what word Mr. Blount threw at him, he pulled himself up straight and, in a loud clear voice, spelled it correctly. Before long, the classroom was buzzing with excitement. Boy oh boy, Willy thought, looking at Cecil in surprise, I bet we win this time.

After the spelling practice, Mr. Blount divided the class into groups. In one corner, four girls were learning to spell words by singing them out to one another. Sarah was sitting by the stove helping five of the youngest mark letters on their slates. On the other side of the stove, Frank and his cronies pretended to work at arithmetic problems. Willy, Cecil and two other boys gathered around the teacher's desk to practise the times-table. "Seven times two makes fourteen," the boys chanted in unison. "Seven times three makes twenty-one, seven times four makes twenty-eight …"

Willy could do the sevens without thinking. His attention started to wander. Out of the corner of his eye he saw a hand reach out and close around Cecil's ornate glass ink bottle. "Seven times nine makes sixty-three," Willy chanted on without missing a beat, but his mind was working furiously. Who was it?

"Seven times twelve makes eighty-four" ended the arithmetic session. On the way back to his bench, Willy darted glances at Frank and his buddies. The smirking faces were dead giveaways.

"My ink bottle," Cecil hissed at him. "And my penknife. I left them right here."

Willy saw the teacher looking their way. "Shh!" he said, and then he spotted the ink bottle. It sat on the hot iron top of the school stove, tightly corked and hissing gently. Before he could get to it, a loud pop broke the silence. Every head swivelled as the cork from the ink bottle hit the ceiling in a splatter of black ink. More ink frothed up over the sides of the bottle and sizzled on the stove top.

Mr. Blount whirled around. "Whose bottle is that?" he bellowed.

Willy stared down at his slate, holding his breath. Mr. Blount wasn't called Basher Blount for nothing.

"That's *my* bottle, sir!" Cecil said indignantly. "But I — "

"Yours! I'm surprised at you, Master Hawthorne, surprised and disappointed. Just because you spelled the whole school down is no reason to think you can get away with such a trick."

Willy couldn't believe his ears. Basher Blount actually believed that Cecil, Sissy Cecil, would dare try that! Willy looked around. Frank had tilted his bench back and was lounging against the wall, grinning broadly. His two cronies smirked beside him. Everyone else had gone still, eyes riveted on Cecil, who sat white-faced and shaking.

"Stand out, Master Hawthorne," Basher Blount said, making his switch whistle through the air. "Stand out."

Frank's going to get away with it, Willy thought, furious. He shot to his feet. "Cecil didn't do it, sir."

"Do you mean to say, William Robertson, that *you* did it?"

Willy paused.

"Well, sir," said the teacher. "I'm waiting." The switch tapped menacingly on the desk. "Who did it?"

When the building was ready, the parents advertised for a teacher. If more than 20 students enrolled, the government would pay 100 dollars a year towards a teacher's salary. The rest came from the parents. The usual fee for each child was 25 cents a month plus a cord of wood in the winter months.

Very few teachers wanted to work in backwoods schools. The pay was not only low, it was often difficult to collect. Money was scarce, so farmers often arrived with produce 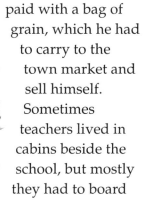 instead. One teacher was paid with a bag of grain, which he had to carry to the town market and sell himself. Sometimes teachers lived in cabins beside the school, but mostly they had to board around, living one month with each family in the neighbourhood. Because conditions were so rough in the early days, most backwoods teachers were men. Some men who became schoolmasters were saving up to buy their own farms. Others were former soldiers unable to do the hard work of clearing land for a farm because of a war wound or other disability.

Books were scarce. The teacher might have one copy of a speller or a reader, sometimes only a Bible. Few children had books to practise reading at home, and many had to miss school to help with farm work. So "book learning" was hit-and-miss.

Discipline was strict in early schools. The teacher kept order with a stick and a sarcastic tongue. Students were beaten for anything from not learning fast enough to being rude to the teacher. Parents didn't object unless the teacher used the stick too harshly. People believed that if you spared the rod, you spoiled the child.

The worst time for the teacher was in the middle of the winter. Then there was little work to do on the farms, and all the big boys came to school. Often the teacher had to fight the biggest boy before the others would behave. If they thought they could get away with it, the bigger boys would lock the teacher out or, worse still, throw him out the door. Being a teacher took muscles as well as brains in those days.

BACKWOODS SCHOLARS

Letters and numbers. That's what most pioneer children learned. They scratched the alphabet onto slates with slate pencils as they learned to write. Later they graduated to homemade ink, quill pens and paper brought from home.

They learned arithmetic that would help them with everyday life. Adding and subtracting were used to figure out their account at the general store. Multiplying and dividing helped them figure out the size of a field or the number of cords in a pile of wood. Children attended school until they were 12 or until they had learned the "rule of three," a method for finding the size of an object too large to measure easily. Early settlers needed to know how to use this rule to find heights of trees and distances across rivers.

This is how the rule of three works: Willy's father was going to cut down a tree near the cabin. To make sure it would not fall on the house and buildings, he needed to know how tall it was.

To find the height of the tree, he wrote:

$$\frac{\text{stick length}}{\text{stick shadow length}} = \frac{\text{tree height}}{\text{tree shadow length}}$$

or

$$\frac{1}{2} = \frac{x}{30}$$

or

$$2x = 30$$

or

$$x = 15 \text{ lengths}$$

So, using the rule of three, Mr. Robertson figured out that the tree was 15 lengths tall. Now he could measure this distance along the ground to see if the tree would fall too close to the cabin.

First he drove a stick into the ground. He measured the length of the stick from the ground up and the length of the stick's shadow. Next he measured the length of the tree's shadow. Now he had the three numbers he needed to find the unknown fourth.

The stick was 1 length long.

Its shadow was 2 lengths long.

The tree's shadow was 30 lengths long.

Pioneer Measuring

How do you measure if you don't have a metre stick or a ruler? A pioneer household had few measuring devices, often only a crude two-foot marker scratched onto an axe handle. For rough measurements, body parts came in handy.

• What size of sticks for kindling? No thicker than your thumb.

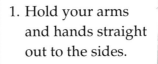

• How big is that horse? Big enough to pull my plough? Oh yes, it's a good 15 hands high.

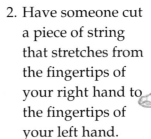

• Buying fabric? Ask for a "cloth yard" — the length of the merchant's out-stretched arm, from his nose to his thumbtip.

If you knew how tall you were, you had another useful measuring device.

Try this.

1. Hold your arms and hands straight out to the sides.

2. Have someone cut a piece of string that stretches from the fingertips of your right hand to the fingertips of your left hand.

3. Put one end of the string on the floor. Does the other end reach the top of your head? Try the same thing with other people. Are most people as tall as their arm span? How could this help you measure?

44

Fox and Geese

The middle of the school day was dinner time. It was also playtime. Schoolyard games then were similar to games now: tag, skipping, crack the whip and ball games (an inflated pig's bladder served as a ball). One pioneer version of tag, called fox and geese, was played in the winter. Here's how to play it.

1. In the snow, mark out a large circle at least 15 m (50 feet) in diameter. Make eight spokes across it and a small circle in the middle, so that it looks like a huge wagon wheel.

2. Choose one person to be the fox. A counting-out rhyme was often used to choose the fox. Everyone stood in a circle holding out one clenched fist. The leader counted around the circle, hitting one fist for each word. The last person to be hit was the fox. One verse goes this way:

Wire, briar, limber
  lock
Three geese in a flock
One flew east, one
  flew west
One flew over the
  cuckoo's nest
O-u-t, out!

3. The fox is "it." He or she chases the geese (the other players) up and down the spokes and around the rim of the circle. If a goose reaches the small inner circle, he or she is home free. When a goose is tagged, he or she becomes the fox.

A MIXED BAG

Children from many different backgrounds met in backwoods schools. Most of the settlers came from England, Ireland and Scotland, but some came from the United States. Many American settlers were Germans from Pennsylvania who left the States during the American Revolution. Some settlers were Black Americans who escaped from plantations in the southern States. A few Jewish settlers came from Europe. Despite the many backgrounds, most settlers worked cooperatively with their neighbours to overcome the hardships of life in the bush.

BABY ANIMALS

"Pa's back!"

Willy buried the blade of his hatchet in the wood block, scattering the kindling he'd been chopping, and ran down to the river, where his father was beaching the canoe. George came thundering in from the field he'd been clearing and the two boys began off-loading crates and baskets.

Pa arched his back, stretched, then put an arm around Ma. "Good to be home," he said, patting Tommy, who was burbling contentedly on Ma's shoulder. Sarah arrived with a mug of cider. "There's my good girl. You know just what I need."

"Did you have any trouble?" Ma asked.

"Never even got my feet wet."

They'd been worrying since yesterday morning when Pa decided to take the canoe down the river, still swollen with winter run-off, rather than trudge along muddy forest trails to the market.

"What did you get?" Lizzie demanded.

Pa grinned. "Baby animals."

Everyone gathered around the load as Willy put the last basket down. Through the slats of a large crate two white geese hissed and snapped. Sarah lifted the lid off another crate. On a bed of straw curled two tiny pink pigs. She scooped one up in her arms. "Isn't it sweet, Lizzie?" The piglet wriggled and squealed as the girls stroked its silky skin. "Here, wrap it in your apron," Sarah said. "We'll play dolls." At least for a week or two, she thought, remembering how quickly the soft, wriggly creature would grow into a ferocious, bristly hog.

"How's the work coming?" Pa asked George. It was always his first question when he came home.

"Cleared the last of the stones, and now I'm grubbing up roots."

"What's that noise?" Willy asked. A sound like the mewling of a new baby came from a covered basket. Pa lifted the lid.

"A puppy!" Willy shouted. He made a grab and the puppy scrabbled away, yipping frantically.

"Be gentle," Ma warned. "Wait till he's used to us."

"What's his name? He looks just like Shep. Even one white ear."

"Doesn't have a name as yet. Came from the same farmer, though. Probably a nephew of Shep's."

"D'ye think Shep will ever come back, Pa?" Willy's question reminded them all of the terrible time in the middle of the winter when they realized their sheepdog had disappeared. Pa and George had tramped through the forest for days, calling and calling. Finally they'd given up.

Pa sighed. "You'll just have to accept it, Willy. If Shep could come home, he would have by now."

Willy looked at the puppy, sniffing around the corners of the basket. "Shep was a right smart dog."

"We'll train this one the way we did Shep. And you can think of a name for him. But right now we need to get these geese into the water."

George was already sliding the crate towards the water's edge. "Stand back," he said. Wedging his knife behind one slat, he pried it loose. The geese rushed out, honking and hissing. Soon they were in the water, paddling around, inspecting their new home.

"Let's get the rest up to the barn," Pa said, and everyone grabbed a basket or one end of a crate.

Willy carried the puppy up the hill in its basket. He stood by the barn, letting the puppy lick his face until Ma called.

"Willy, I need that kindling."

"Stay in your basket, now. I'll be back soon."

By the time he'd run to the cabin with his load and hurried back, the puppy had tipped himself out of the basket and was bumbling around on stubby legs. Earlier, Sarah had scattered crushed corn, and Ma's four hens were swishing about the yard, busily pecking it up. A handful of chicks tumbled after one hen, their yellow down just giving way to brown and white speckled feathers. The puppy lolloped after them, nudging them into line with his nose. A hen clucked at him, but the puppy stood his ground, yipping back at her. Suddenly, with a rush of wings, the rooster swooped. The puppy scrambled for cover, squeezing under the porch just as the rooster's beak slashed down.

Willy stamped and flapped his hands at the rooster. "Shoo! Shoo!" Tossing his red comb triumphantly, the rooster strutted back to his little band.

"Come on out. You're safe now." Willy lay down and reached under the porch. Needle-sharp teeth nipped him. Under his hands he could feel the wild thumping of the puppy's heart. "You're scared, aren't you?" He loosened his hold. "Guess you never met anything as fierce as that rooster." The puppy lay panting, watching Willy suck at the bead of blood on his finger. "Tell you what, you little nipper, I'll get you some milk."

The puppy was still under the porch when Willy came back. He slid the bowl right up to the puppy's nose. It twitched inquiringly. Then the puppy hunched up and began to lap. Slowly Willy inched the bowl out and the puppy followed. He licked up the last drop, then turned to inspect Willy's toes.

"Hey, little nipper," Willy said, waving a stick. "I'm going to teach you to fetch." The puppy obligingly snapped at the stick. "No, wait till I throw it." The puppy growled and tossed his head, trying to wrestle the stick out of Willy's hand. Hanging onto the stick, they tumbled over and over. "You're supposed to do what I tell you," Willy laughed.

The new gander came waddling up the slope, picking at grass. The puppy's ears pricked up. He swivelled to look, yipped once or twice as though saying, "Get back down to the water," then trotted purposefully towards the startled bird.

The gander arched his neck and hissed. Willy ran down the slope and scooped the puppy up in his arms. "You know what you're supposed to do, don't you, Nipper," he crowed. "You're just itching to get out there and herd." He laughed as the puppy licked enthusiastically at his face. "But you'd better listen to what I'm telling you about ganders or you'll be right sorry when *you* get nipped."

FARM ANIMALS

Wintering over livestock was difficult on a backwoods pioneer farm. Barns were too small to store much feed and too cold and drafty to protect small animals. The Robertsons managed to feed and shelter two cows, two oxen, six sheep and some hens each winter. Everything else had to be bought in the spring from farmers closer to towns.

Geese were one of the most useful barnyard creatures. Their large quill feathers were made into pens. Two or three times a summer Mrs. Robertson and Granny would pluck the geese for feathers to make pillows and warm mattresses. Plucking didn't hurt the geese, it just made them angry. To keep a goose from pecking, Mrs. Robertson slipped a sock over its head, then held the body between her knees.

When geese weighed about 5 kg (11 pounds), they were ready for market. The Robertsons sold some of their geese, but most of their small flock were used for their own food. As a goose roasted on a spit Mrs. Robertson carefully caught the drippings in a pan. Goose grease was good for rubbing on wheezy chests and helped soften hands and cheeks chapped by the cold.

Hens were a source of food and money. Once the family's needs were met, extra eggs could be sold at the general store and extra chickens could be sold at the market. Egg money belonged to the women of the family because they looked after the flock.

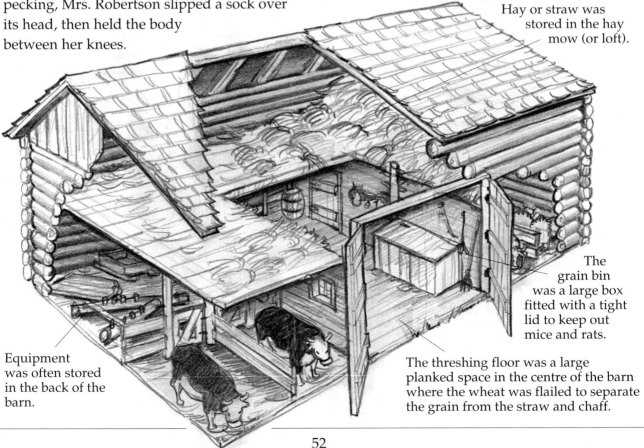

Hay or straw was stored in the hay mow (or loft).

The grain bin was a large box fitted with a tight lid to keep out mice and rats.

Equipment was often stored in the back of the barn.

The threshing floor was a large planked space in the centre of the barn where the wheat was flailed to separate the grain from the straw and chaff.

Keeping the hens and rooster alive and safe was difficult on a backwoods farm. The Robertsons built a hen house up against the barn, but on the coldest days of winter Mrs. Robertson brought her birds into the house to keep them warm. When the hens were sitting on clutches of eggs, they were often attacked by skunks, weasels, minks and foxes. Hawks swooped on hens running about the yard. Although the rooster valiantly fought all these predators, every so often a hen or some of the chicks would be carried off.

Hens fed themselves by scratching in the dirt for bugs and seeds. The family helped start egg production in the spring by scattering corn and bran. Sometimes they mixed in ashes and lime to harden the eggshells, so that the eggs were easier to store.

Through the summer the hogs rooted for their food in the woods or anywhere they could find a tasty morsel — including the farmer's cornfields if he hadn't made his fences "hog tight." Mr. Robertson trained the hogs to stay near the farm buildings, safe from marauding bears, by putting out slops (leftover food and buttermilk) for them. Early in the fall the children gathered baskets of acorns and beechnuts to fatten the hogs for butchering day.

In the early days, dogs and cats were hard to come by. Farmers in the backwoods counted on an itinerant pedlar carrying the odd kitten or puppy in his pack, or they might find one for sale at the market.

Every farm needed a watchdog to warn of strangers and to chase prowling foxes and other barnyard predators. Every family wanted a cat who was a good mouser to keep vermin (rats and mice) out of the wheat. Sometimes cats and dogs got lost in the woods and turned wild. The dogs, in particular, became a menace. During the winter, when finding food was difficult, wild dogs often attacked travellers in the woods. In telling the story later, the victims often blamed wolves, giving them a bad reputation.

Hen-house Mystery

One morning, Mr. Robertson awoke to find tracks outside the hen house. He didn't need to go inside to find what had happened. He could tell from the clues. Study the tracks and see if you can figure it out. Answer on page 238.

fox   weasel   skunk

FENCES

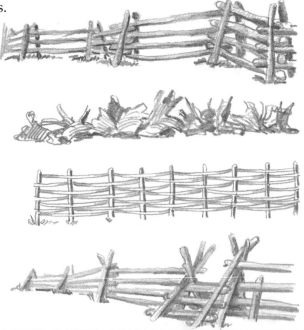

Horse high, hog tight and skunk-proof!" That's the kind of fence a backwoods farmer needed — a barrier to keep his precious crops safe from hungry animals.

A split-rail fence might be straight or crooked (called a snake fence).

Stumps made a long-lasting fence that kept cattle and sheep in their places.

A wattle fence woven from willow branches kept deer and hares out of the vegetable garden.

A stile made crossing a fence easier.

SPRING WORK

Spring was a busy time of year. In a few short weeks the family had to plant wheat, corn and potato crops to feed themselves over the coming year. They planted more wheat than they needed so that they could sell the excess at the market or to the grist mill owner. Money from this sale was needed to pay their taxes and to buy salt and other necessities.

CLEARING THE LAND

No planting could be done until the land was cleared. First the area was underbrushed — all the bushes and small trees were cut down and piled for burning. This gave a chopper room to swing his axe and cut down the larger trees. One man could underbrush 0.4 ha (an acre) of forest in six days.

Next, the farmer and his sons or hired men chopped down the trees. The fallen trees were chopped or sawn into 3-m (10-foot) lengths to make them easier to move. Some of the trunks were dragged away by oxen to be used for building or fence-making. The rest were burned with the brushwood. On average, a settler could clear 9 ha (22 acres) in the first three years. The work was so hard that neighbours often held "bees" and worked together to help one another clear the land.

Ashes from the burnings were collected in barrels and sold to soap factories. This was an important source of money for the early settlers.

Once cleared of trees, the field was still full of roots and covered with stumps. The roots could be grubbed out with a mattock (a kind of axe), but the stumps were so difficult to remove that the first crops were planted around them. Over the years, the stumps were cleared away one by one. Some were pulled out by oxen, some were shattered with gunpowder, others were just left to rot.

Boulders also had to be dug or pried out and hauled away on a stoneboat. It took many years to create today's smooth, level farm fields.

PLANTING

As soon as the fields were dry, usually about the beginning of May, planting began. Fields that still had roots were harrowed. To do this, a team of oxen pulled a heavy wooden frame with sharp teeth over the land. This scratched the surface of the soil so that seeds could be sown. Fields cleared of roots were ploughed to loosen the soil.

To sow wheat, barley or oats, the farmer walked over the land, scattering handfuls of seeds to the right and left. This method, called broadcasting, wasted seed but was the only method backwoods farmers had until seeding machines became available.

After the seed had been broadcast, the early settler tied a large branch to the oxen's yoke. The oxen dragged it over the sown ground, scuffling earth over the seeds. From then on, the farmer hoped for a mixture of sun and rain to give him a good harvest.

Farmers saved the best of their crop each year to use as seed the next year. If damp or mildew spoiled the seed, they had to buy more at the market or from a neighbour, something many couldn't afford to do.

harrowing

ploughing

broadcasting

Grow a Potato Plant

Potatoes were often a settler's first crop. They could be planted among the stumps of a newly cleared field and would be the major source of food for the coming winter. Before planting, potatoes kept for seed were cut into pieces, each containing an eye from which the new plant would grow.

You'll need:
- 4 toothpicks
- a sprouted potato
- a glass filled with water
- a planting pot
- potting soil

1. Stick the toothpicks into the potato and rest it on the rim of the glass as shown. The sprouted eye of the potato should be in the water.
2. Place the glass on a windowsill. Keep the water level high so that the sprouted part is always in water.
3. In a few weeks you should see roots emerge from the bottom. Shortly afterwards, the top will split and a shoot (stem) will begin to grow upwards. When the plant sprouts its first leaves, remove the toothpicks and carefully transfer the potato to a pot containing soil. Plant it deep enough to cover all the roots. Place your plant near a sunny window.

CORN

Corn was one of the most useful plants the early settlers grew. The kernels could be boiled to make porridge or ground to make flour and cornmeal. The stalks were stored to make winter feed for the animals. The husks were dried to stuff into mattresses or braided to make mats. The cobs were burned to a white ash and used as a form of baking powder or thrown on the fire when hams were being cured. Cobs were also cut into chunks to make bottle corks or checkers pieces, used as spools for winding thread and dressed up to make dolls. Pieces of dried cobs were used as toilet paper.

When the oak leaves were the size of a squirrel's ear, the settlers knew it was time to plant the corn. This was often done by the women and children.

One person hoed up a hill of earth and another dropped six seeds into each hill, then scuffed a bare foot across the hole to cover the seeds.

Often, the children passed the time by chanting:

One for the blackbird
One for the crow
One for the cutworm
And three to grow.

A few weeks later, when the first leaves had sprouted, settlers planted pumpkin seeds around the corn. As the pumpkin vines spread, they smothered the weeds.

Settlers learned about corn from Native people. Iroquois women, in particular, were experts at growing corn. They chose the plumpest and biggest kernels from the previous summer's harvest for seed. These kernels were soaked in herbal teas to make them sprout faster. Before the women planted the kernels, they dropped a small fish into each hole for fertilizer. Later in the season, they planted squash or pumpkin and bean seeds around each corn plant. Beans, squash and corn were called "the three sisters" because they helped each other. The beans and squash added nutrients to the soil for the corn; the corn stalk provided a pole for the beans to grow up; and the squash plant spread over the ground, smothering the weeds.

STORING THE CORN

Pioneer corn was flint corn, a much tougher variety than the sweet corn we eat today. One of the children scraped the kernels off the cob and spread them out to dry. Then Mrs. Robertson stored the dried corn in linen sacks or wooden kegs until she needed it for cooking. She had to boil the flint corn in a weak solution of lye, to loosen the outer casing, before she could make a porridge called hominy. To make cornmeal, she ground the dried kernels in a small coffee grinder. The cornmeal could be boiled to make a pudding called supporne or baked into a bread called johnny cake. Corn dried on the cob was stored in a corn crib. It was used to feed the animals. The crib was a bin with open slats that let the air through. Tin shields on the crib's legs kept mice from climbing in.

The best ears were saved as seed corn. To keep them over the winter, Mr. Robertson peeled back the husks, braided them and hung the ears in the barn to dry.

FINDING A HONEY TREE

One day in the middle of April, Sarah stepped out the cabin door into warm sunshine. On her hip she balanced a wooden bowl full of dirty dishwater, which she emptied into the hedge surrounding Granny's herb garden. She stood for a moment looking out across the still-brown fields. In the distance she saw someone. A visitor? Then she recognized the burly figure of their neighbour, old Mr. Burkholder, and her heart jumped.

"Is this the day, Uncle Jacob?" she called.

"This is the day, young'un." Jacob Burkholder's eyes twinkled as he held up a small wooden box. "Here I am, all ready with my bee trap."

Old Mr. Burkholder had lived in the backwoods all his life, and he was happy to show his neighbours some of the tricks he'd learned. One was how to find honey.

Still carrying the bowl, Sarah ran towards the barn. "Willy, Willy, come quick. Uncle Jacob's here. We're going bee hunting." Before she reached the barn door, her father and George appeared.

"Mornin', Jacob," Pa said. "All's well with you?"

Ma and Meg appeared at the cabin door. A visitor provided a welcome break. "Will you have some coffee with us, Jacob?" Ma called.

"That'd be right nice."

"Wait! Wait! Don't go yet!" The frantic wail came from the river bank, where Willy was struggling to hoist a full bucket out of the water.

"Don't fret yourself, young'un," Uncle Jacob called. "We'll bide till you're ready."

Sarah sped down the slope to her brother and grabbed the rope handle. "Here, I'll help you." Together they hefted the bucket up the path and onto the porch. The grown-ups had already disappeared inside.

"I thought he'd forgotten," Willy panted, flopping onto the step.

"He said the first warm, sunny day," Sarah reminded him. "And this is it."

It seemed an eternity before Uncle Jacob appeared in the doorway. "No trouble at all," he assured Ma and Pa. "Got to make sure we satisfy that sweet tooth of Willy's. Too bad about Sarah not liking sweets," he teased, sitting down beside her on the edge of the porch.

"Well now, young'uns," he said, pulling a small wooden box from his jacket pocket. "Here's what I brought." He opened it to show a piece of honeycomb and a flat stone. "Now we'll need a little pot full of hot coals and, Willy, that red scarf I saw you wearing this winter." Sarah ran for the coals and Willy for the scarf, then the three bee-hunters set off.

Near the river, where the sun was warming an open grassy meadow, Uncle Jacob stopped. "Bees'll be good and hungry this early in the year," he told the children. "So we're going to make them a little treat."

He dropped the flat stone into the pot of coals. Soon it was too hot to touch. Using two sticks as tongs, he lifted the stone out and set it on the ground. Next, he smeared some of the honeycomb over the rock. The waxy honeycomb melted, sending up an aroma that made Sarah's mouth water. Just like pull taffy! she thought.

"Bees can smell that a mile away," the old man chuckled. "Bring 'em here in no time."

He put the open wooden box on the ground beside the rock. "Here, Sarah, pour a little of that honey in. And Willy, when I give the sign I want you to close the box. But first, we wait." He settled himself on a fallen log.

A few minutes later Sarah heard a quiet buzzing. Uncle Jacob put his finger to his lips, and they watched silently as a bee landed in the honey box. Willy crept forward and slid the lid over the box. "Now what?" he whispered.

"We give it time to eat its fill of honey, then let it out and follow it," said Uncle Jacob. "My old grandpa called it 'coursing the bee.'"

Uncle Jacob opened the box. "Now watch carefully where it heads." The bee rose slowly into the air, circled three times, then zoomed away. "Quick, it's making a beeline for home."

They ran across the field towards the woods. "It's gone," Sarah wailed. "I can't see it."

"No matter. We'll just stop here and do it all over again. Now we know the direction and the bee knows there's food. Just you wait. It'll be back and a bunch of others with it. We'll be coursing again in no time."

Uncle Jacob reheated his bait on the hot rock and back the bees came. This time the hunters were successful. In no time, they tracked the bees to an old tree humming with activity.

"Now we'll put your mark on it, young Wilhelm," Uncle Jacob said as he tied Willy's scarf around the tree. "Come fall, when it's full of honey, you'll know how to find it. Meantime, everyone else will know this tree belongs to Sarah and Willy."

THE SWEET SMELL OF SUCCESS

Finding a bee tree was a lot of work. Why go to all that trouble? Honey was one of the few sweeteners available in the backwoods. White sugar was expensive and had to be bought in town. Making maple sugar took even more work than finding a bee tree. So early settlers were always delighted to find a honey tree, either by accident or because they knew the habits of bees.

The successful bee-hunter usually chose a day in early spring, when the bees had few flowers to tempt them and when they would be particularly hungry after the long winter. Because bees rarely roam more than 3 km (2 miles) from home, the hunter knew he wouldn't have a long trek to the hive. When bees are full, they make a "beeline" — as straight a line as the countryside will permit — for home. But bees can disappear quickly among trees, so the hunter knew he'd have to set out his bait two or three times. Once he found the honey tree, the hunter marked it, then left it alone until the bees had filled it with honey.

In the fall, the Robertsons loaded crocks and bowls and tubs onto a sled and went back out to Willy and Sarah's tree. They also took hot coals in a big iron kettle. By putting wet leaves or cedar boughs on the coals, they made thick smoke to calm the bees, making them sleepy and less likely to sting. Then the boys cut the tree down and everyone scooped as much of the honeycomb as possible into the bowls and crocks. Not all the bees were "smoked," so there were some stings. But there were also sticky fingers to lick clean. Sarah and Willy felt very sick that night from gorging themselves on honey. But the result was worth the stings and the sickness — enough honey to last the winter and beeswax to make a few precious candles!

64

What about the bees? Their winter food was gone and many of them died. Early settlers didn't know how to take the honey without destroying the hive. Gradually they learned how to keep swarms of bees on their farms in hives made of coiled straw, called skeps, or in hollow logs called beegums. Even with these movable beehives, the only way to harvest the honey was to cut out all the combs, leaving no food, and again most of the bees died. Not until the late 1850s did someone invent a beehive with sliding frames, which made it possible for bee-keepers to take some of the honey and leave the rest to feed the bees through the winter.

Sweet Treats and Remedies

For a tasty pioneer snack, mix 250 mL (1 cup) of honey with 50 mL (1/4 cup) of butter. Spread some on toast or a tea biscuit. Store the rest of the honey butter in the refrigerator.

The next time you have a cough, mix the juice of one lemon and 15 mL (1 tablespoon) of honey in 125 mL (1/2 cup) of hot water. Drink slowly. For a sore throat, let a teaspoonful of liquid honey trickle down your throat and coat the sore spot.

Pioneers used honey as a salve for scrapes and small cuts. Scientists now know that honey contains an ingredient that works as an antibiotic (a substance that slows down the growth of germs).

beegum

skep

BEE LORE

There are thousands of kinds of bees, but only a few make and store honey. True honeybees didn't exist in North America until the 1600s. Europeans who settled in New England and Virginia brought them on their ships. Swarms of honeybees escaped into the forests and gradually moved north and west, as far as the prairies. Native people soon learned to harvest wild honey and taught the later settlers how to find bee trees.

The bee Sarah and Willy followed into the woods was a worker. In her six weeks of life she makes hundreds of flights and carries enough nectar back to the hive to make a teaspoonful of honey.

The hive contains as many as 70 000 other bees, all living together in a nest made of beeswax combs built by the bees themselves.

Most of the bees are workers, each with a special task. Some guard the entrance to the hive, some act as nurses and feed the brood (larvae about to become adult bees), others clean the hive. But the major job of the workers is to collect nectar and pollen.

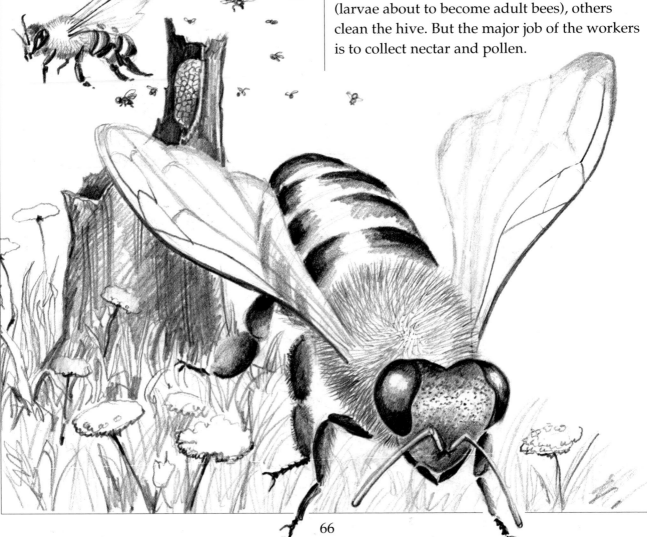

Pollen is yellow powder gathered from the anthers of flowers. The bee kneads the pollen into a little ball and tucks it into a cavity in its hind leg to carry it back to the hive. There, nurse bees mix it with honey to feed the bee larvae.

Nectar is a sweet liquid gathered from the centres of flowers. The worker bee stores the nectar in her honey sac, where it mixes with saliva. This causes chemical changes that turn the nectar into honey.

Back at the hive, the bee empties the liquid from her honey sac into wax cells, where other bees fan it with their wings to reduce the moisture. Then the cell is capped with wax to keep the honey fresh until it is needed for food.

Each hive has one queen and a number of drones, or male bees, whose only function is to mate with the queen. After the mating flight the drones die and the queen goes back inside the hive to lay thousands of eggs.

Be Sting Smart

You're most likely to see (or hear) bees and other buzzing insects when you've spread out a tasty picnic lunch. How scared should you be? Not very. Here are some tips to help you spot the stingers, so that you can stay clear of them:

Wasp
Very persistent around food. Will sting if annoyed.

Honeybee
Will sting only if it feels endangered. Important because it pollinates flowers.

Bumblebee
Very reluctant to sting. Much bigger than a honeybee. Hairy black coat marked with yellow. Important because it pollinates flowers. Does not make honey: it eats nectar as it takes it from the flowers.

Hoverfly
Mimics the way a bee hovers in front of a flower. Same striping as a bee. This protective colouring makes it look dangerous but it has no stinger. To tell it from a bee, count the wings. A bee has four, the hoverfly only two.

GRANNY'S STORY

Sarah shifted and fidgeted on her hard stump stool. They'd been sitting under the rowan tree for ages, while Granny picked over her seed collection.

"What's this one?" Sarah lifted a tiny linen pouch out of Granny's basket and peered in at the fine black seeds.

"Horehound." Granny didn't look up from the little bags she was sorting. "Cured your sore throat last winter, ye'll recall. No, don't put it there. It's last year's seed."

"Why do you save so much? You never use it all."

"Never plant all your seeds or you're sure to go hungry. First planting might be wiped out. Learned that years ago from *my* old gran." Granny dropped five pouches into her apron pocket. "Here's the ones we want. Come along and we'll see what that brother of yours has made of the garden."

Trailing rakes and a hoe, Sarah followed Granny around the back of the cabin. On the slope leading up to the new house was a small garden hedged in with currant bushes.

"Ah, that's the laddie, George. Just the way I like it."

George grinned, shouldered his spade and marched off, whistling.

"Now let's have a feel of this soil." Granny scooped up a handful and rubbed both palms together. "See how it makes nice little balls? And how it crumbles when I rub it through my fingers? Try it yourself, Sarah, so you'll get the feel of good earth."

Sarah ran her fingers through the loosened soil. It felt warm and left a smell on her hands like secret, shady places under logs.

"Aye, 'tis good earth, but it's not like the earth I brought from Scotland. Did I ever tell you about that?"

Shall I say yes or no, Sarah wondered. She'd heard all of Granny's stories, but sometimes new bits were added. And a good story made work go faster. "Tell me," she said.

"Where's that wee rake your father made? I'll tell you while we smooth out this patch."

They worked for a while in silence, Sarah breaking up the big lumps with a hoe while Granny ran the rake over the surface.

"Such a long time ago." Granny sighed and leaned on her rake. "Your father was only eight, younger than you. I remember I was out spinning under the rowan tree to catch the last of the light when my old gran came hobbling up the path.

"'So you're flitting,' she said.

"I was near to crying trying to explain to her how there'd been no work for a year now. Leaving home for the new world seemed our only hope.

"'Well, what can't be cured must be endured — but you'll not go without the luck of the house,' she said, patting the rowan tree.

"I couldn't believe my ears — take a tree on a ship across an ocean? But she was right — I did want to take a slip from the rowan tree that guarded the door of our cottage.

"'Where there's a will there's a way,' she reminded me and that gave me hope." Granny leaned on the rake and stared off into the distance.

"And then what?" Sarah asked.

"Oh, she outs with her knife and takes slips from my rowan tree. By the time we left Scotland, six months later, we had two nice wee trees in crockery pots, growing in good Scottish earth. My gran wanted to make sure we'd always have a handful of home."

Granny stood back and looked at the garden. "Well, that's nice and smooth. Take this stick and make some rows while I dribble in the seed. We'll put tansy here."

For the next few minutes Sarah concentrated on drawing perfectly straight lines across the garden. "Tell the next bit — about the crossing."

"Och, what a trial that was! We'd been warned the sea captain might be a scoundrel, so we'd taken our own food. Sacks of oatmeal and our own barrel of flour. And sure enough, the food on board that ship wasna fit to give a pig. But it was the water that near did us in. Smelled like sewer water it did. I boiled our ration every day. Some went for the oatmeal, some to water my wee trees and the rest we drank."

"How could you bear it, if it tasted so awful?"

"What choice did we have? Three weeks at sea we were. Still three to go and what did that scoundrel do? Cut our water ration in half. And that wasn't the end of it. In half again the next week. Three measures a day for six people, that's all we were given. What with the oatmeal to make and wee bairns that didna understand why they couldn't have more to drink, I was in despair. And my trees! I wanted so badly to bring that little bit of Scotland to the new land, but I couldn't take water from my bairns.

"Well, one day I was poking at the soil around the roots — dry as death it was and the leaves all drooping. My wee Robbie was sitting watching me. I remember telling him they wouldn't make it. 'Where there's a will, there's a way, Mam,' Robbie chirps, then he dashes off and in the blink of an eye he's back with his tin cup half full of water. 'Where did ye get that?' I gasped. 'Coaxed a little from this one and a little from that one,' he says, and every day for the rest of the trip he managed to come up with water to keep my trees alive."

Sarah always liked the part where her father was the hero. She gave the earth over the seeds a satisfied pat. "But that wasn't the end of the story," she prompted.

"We settled down in Nova Scotia and my trees flourished," Granny continued. "And we flourished, too. Ah, there's always a calm before the storm. We'd cleared a good bit of land and the lads were nearly grown. One day they were all out ploughing. The blade caught on a tree root, the handle whipped out of your grandad's hand and smashed into his chest." Granny leaned on the rake, a brooding look on her face. "He never healed properly," she said at last. "It wasna three months till he was gone.

"I'll never forget the day we buried him, on land he owned — that eased my heart some. We were standing by the grave and the minister saying the last words over him and me thinking he should be put in Scottish ground alongside his ma and his pa and the two bairns we buried back home. I felt a strong arm around me, my Robbie, a braw laddie by then. He took my hand and poured some dirt in it. 'From the rowan tree, Ma,' he said. 'A little bit of Scotland to bury him with.' I could hardly see for the tears. I scattered that good earth on his coffin and I knew, I just knew, he felt more comfortable for having that wee bit of home with him."

Sarah pictured it all in her mind, the tall uncles carrying the coffin, her granny's hand opening to let the earth fall.

"Did you bring some Scottish earth here?"

Granny stopped raking and cocked her head towards Sarah. "No, no, I didn't," she said slowly. "I made sure to bring slips from my rowan trees, but … I'll tell you a feeling that's come over me lately, Sarah." She stooped and picked up a handful of the freshly tilled soil. "After all these years of working it — it won't be such a bad thing, when the time comes, to have *this* earth thrown on my coffin."

THE LONG VOYAGE

Granny Robertson grew up in a village in Scotland. As a young girl she spun wool, along with her mother and sisters, for her father and brothers to weave into cloth. Many men in their part of Scotland were trained as weavers. When she was 18, Granny married a young weaver from a neighbouring village, and they set up house in a two-room stone cottage — one room for the family and one room for the loom. From that village and many others like it, hundreds of lengths of woollen tartan were sent to the cities for sale.

By the time the Robertsons had a young family, times were hard. Gradually the woollen factories took work away from the home weavers. One autumn day, a man from the Settlers' Society called a meeting in the schoolhouse. He talked about the free land and good opportunities in America. Uprooting a family was a scary idea, but the Robertsons were more worried about finding work in Scotland. Finally they decided they would have to take the chance.

They bought tickets on a ship that was leaving the following April. All winter they planned and packed. Letters from friends in Canada warned them to bring warm clothes and good stout boots. Pewter dishes, iron pots and frying pans were stowed into two big boxes.

Granny packed her spinning wheel and Grandad his wooden loom so they could make their own cloth again once they had sheep. Everything else was sold — their furniture, their chickens and pigs, even their few china dishes.

Settlers travelled to America by ship. Few had seen a sailing ship before they arrived at the dock. The living quarters were cramped.

The Robertsons had three bunks for six people and a narrow aisle to store their boxes. If they wanted privacy, they hung blankets in front of their bunks.

Granny Robertson and her family were lucky they had brought their own food with them. Many had no money to buy extra food and spent the six weeks eating ship's biscuit, a rock-hard bread often full of weevils. Some were weak from years of poor food. In the crowded ships they caught diseases such as typhoid fever and died.

Many people were seasick, no one had enough water to wash properly, and the toilets were just pails that were emptied overboard every day. Before long, the smell below deck was unbearable. If the weather was fine, the passengers escaped onto the deck for fresh air and exercise. But often the weather was rough and the hatches were battened (tied) down to keep out the sea water. If the weather was very rough, the passengers weren't allowed to light candles for fear of fire, so they had to huddle in the dark, in the wildly pitching ship, wondering if they would survive.

After six to nine weeks of this, they heard the welcome cry "Land ho!" The first part of their adventure had ended. The second part, finding a new home, was about to begin.

MILKING

Get along, Beauty! Get along!" Willy flicked the cow with the switch he had broken from a tree. "Hurry up, you stupid critter!"

Beauty ambled stubbornly ahead, refusing to be hurried, pausing every so often to browse on spring leaves, paying no heed to the puppy, who was nipping and yipping at her heels. Willy swatted at the mosquitoes that zoomed under the brim of his straw hat to feast at his sweating hairline. "Stupid, stupid, stupid critter," he droned, giving the cow's rump a slap. Why is it always *me* that has to get her? At least they were out of the woods and the barn was in sight.

"There you are! What kept you?" Meg sounded exasperated. Everyone was cross in this unexpectedly hot May. Flies buzzed around the bucket at Meg's feet. She had covered it with a cloth to keep the milk clean and was waiting, hands on hips, while Willy urged the cow along the path. Bessie was already browsing in the night yard, a small fenced-in pasture where the cows were kept overnight to be ready for milking first thing in the morning.

"Wasn't my fault. She'd gone right into the woods. Hidden herself in those alders down by the stream. Couldn't hear her bell. Took ages to find her." Willy thought about the cool water running over his sweaty feet, the little bark boats he'd sent racing with the current, the tadpoles he'd almost caught. No need to tell Meg about that! "Why doesn't she come for the horn?" he grumbled. "Bessie does."

"Just ornery, I guess. Like some people I know. Now, fetch that stool. We'll see if you remember what I've been teaching you."

"What — *now*? I'm hot."

"We're *all* hot," Meg snapped.

"Why can't Sarah do it? I fetched the cow home. Anyway, I'm supposed to be helping George muck out the stables."

"That'll be waiting when you're finished here," Meg said, uncovering the wooden bucket to set it under the cow. "Time you learned to milk. Now get over here and practise."

Willy kicked the cedar block they used as a milking stool until it rolled over to where Beauty stood stamping and blowing.

"Be careful. She plays tricks."

Willy flumped down, scowling. He rubbed his sweaty hands down his pant legs, then reached under the cow. Beauty shifted away. Willy followed, lugging the stool. "Stand still," he ordered, as the cow stamped impatiently and twitched her long tail.

"Watch out, now," Meg warned. "She'll step on your foot as soon as look at you. Lean your head into her side and take hold firmly so she knows you're in charge."

Willy took hold firmly. He squeezed and stroked, just as Meg had shown him. Nothing happened.

"Now what?"

"Try again."

He tried again. Suddenly he realized the cow was crowding closer. She'll have me right off the stool in a minute, ornery thing. Gritting his teeth, Willy put his head down and butted. "Get over!" He pushed his head firmly into the cow's side, struggling to milk at the same time. His hands were aching by the time he finally heard the hiss of milk hitting the side of the pail.

"I did it! Look, Meg." He sat up, taking his head away from the cow's side. Instantly, Beauty stepped sideways and sent him sprawling off the stool.

"Watch out for the milk!" Meg grabbed the bucket. "Get over, Beauty. Get over!"

As Willy scrambled to his feet, the cow's tail lashed out, landing a sharp slap on his bare neck. Tears sprang to his eyes. Miserable beast! He rubbed at the stinging welt.

"Poor Willy," Meg laughed. "You'll catch on. And she'll get used to you sooner or later."

Willy glared at the cow, now standing placidly as Meg sent streams of milk foaming into the bucket. "Just you wait, Beauty. Just you wait."

THE FAMILY COW

As soon as a pioneer family had cleared a little land, they bought a cow. This useful animal provided milk to feed the family and calves that could be sold, slaughtered for meat or, if male, trained to plough and pull a wagon. The milk could also be turned into cheese and butter to trade at the general store or used to fatten the pigs and hens. Very little of the milk was used for drinking. As a result, people didn't get as much calcium as they needed, and many had lost their teeth by the age of 30.

What was Little Miss Muffet doing on her tuffet? Eating cheese curds before they were made into hard cheese. This was a tasty and nutritious treat for pioneer children — just like eating cottage cheese.

The best way to ruin butter is to let cows browse on garlic, wild onions (leeks) or turnips. These give the butter a strong, unpleasant taste.

If a pioneer family ran out of candles, they could melt butter and pour it into a small lamp called a cruisie or betty lamp. The melted butter fuelled the linen wick and gave a small amount of light.

In winter, when cows couldn't browse on fresh grass, the butter made from their milk was almost white. To give the butter a more pleasing colour, carrot scrapings were added.

Families on the move made butter by hanging a leather bag full of cream from the back of the wagon. The bumpy ride churned the butter as the family travelled.

MILKING

Cows produce milk to feed their calves. When a calf is five days old, the mother cow can be milked by the farmer. For the next ten months she will produce much more milk than her calf needs. Pioneer farmers were lucky to get 20 L (21 quarts) of milk a week from each cow. Today, because cows are fed on a carefully balanced diet that includes grains as well as hay and grass, farmers expect at least 10 L (11 quarts) per day.

then   now

Everyone on a pioneer farm learned to milk, but the dairy was most often looked after by women and girls. They had to learn the gentle rhythm that coaxed the milk from the teats. Cows who were upset or uncomfortable wouldn't let their milk down. Milking was done first thing in the morning so the cows could browse in the cool of the day, when the dew was still on the grass, and then find a shady spot to rest and chew their cud (redigest their food) during the hot afternoon. By evening they were ready to be milked again.

Cows milked at the same time every day got used to coming in at the sound of a horn or bell. If a cow had recently had a calf she would come in at the sound of her penned-up baby bleating for milk. Other cows were just plain stubborn and had to be fetched every day. This was a chore for young children and the farm dog. In pioneer days, many children were lost in the woods while searching for stray cows.

MAKING BUTTER

Do you like butter on your toast? Enough to spend 30 minutes making it? On a pioneer farm, the only way to get butter was by churning milk. What does churning do? Milk contains fat globules wrapped in a protein coating. Churning breaks the coating so that the fat globules can stick together. The result: butter.

Making tasty butter meant first leaving fresh milk out in a shallow pan overnight so that the cream would rise to the surface. The next morning the cream was skimmed off with a wooden spoon. Then the cream was left to sit until its surface was shiny and it was slightly sour. Believe it or not, sour cream makes tastier butter than sweet cream. Good butter-makers could tell by looking at the cream when it was ready to churn. In winter the cream would have to sit for several days in front of the fire; in summer, it would only need to sit overnight.

The cream was poured into the churn, and one of the children was given the chore of pounding the dasher rhythmically up and down. The dasher was a stick with paddles on the bottom. It agitated the fat globules, breaking the protein casing and making them stick together. After 15 minutes of churning, the cream started to feel heavy. After another 15 minutes the cream separated into buttermilk and grain-sized pellets of butter.

This back-breaking job was often done by children as young as ten. To keep the rhythm and to make the time pass more quickly, they sometimes sang this song:

> *Come, butter, come*
> *Come, butter, come*
> *Peter standing at the gate*
> *Waiting for a butter cake*
> *Come, butter, come.*

The buttermilk was drained off and saved for baking or fed to the pigs. The butter was put into a bowl and rinsed thoroughly with several changes of cold water. If all the buttermilk was not washed out, the butter would quickly turn rancid. To get rid of the last of the rinse water, the butter was squeezed against the sides of the bowl with a wooden butter paddle, then worked into a lump. Finally it was sprinkled with salt to keep it from spoiling, pressed into a crock and stored in a cool place. If the family didn't have a root cellar, they set the crock on a ledge partway down the well or buried it in the ground.

Make Your Own Butter

Butter making took a lot of time and energy, so the early settlers looked for ways of making it easier. They designed churns that could be turned with a handle or a foot pedal. A glass jar with a screw-top lid was used to make small amounts of butter. Make your own butter using the shake-in-a-jar method.

You'll need:
- 250 mL (1 cup) whipping cream at room temperature
- a small jar with a secure lid
- a bowl
- a wooden spoon

1. Pour the whipping cream into the jar.

2. Screw the lid on and shake the jar vigorously. After about ten minutes, you'll notice that your cream has separated into a bluish-white liquid (buttermilk) and pale yellow clumps of fat (butter).

3. Pour the butter and buttermilk into a bowl.

4. Carefully pour off the buttermilk.

5. Wash the butter with cold water.

6. Press the butter against the side of the bowl with a wooden spoon (metal spoils the taste of the butter), and rinse with water until the water is clear. This gets rid of the last of the buttermilk.

7. Taste the butter. Does it taste like butter from the store? Work in a little salt and taste again.

Shaking the jar serves the same function as dashing the paddle up and down in the wooden churn: it breaks down the membranes or casings of protein around the globules of fat and makes them stick together. The more you shake the jar, the more clusters of fat globules stick together. Soon you have a large lump, instead of many tiny particles suspended throughout the liquid.

MAKING CHEESE

Milk was hard to keep in the days before iceboxes or refrigerators. Turning it into cheese and butter was one way of keeping it over the winter. Cheese was much more difficult to make than butter, but it kept longer. Every summer, when the cows were giving the most milk, Mrs. Robertson would make enough cheese to carry the family through the winter.

She saved 4 L (1 gallon) of milk from each of the morning and evening milkings and let it stand overnight. The next morning she soaked a small piece of rennet in half a cup of water. Rennet, made from the dried stomach of a newborn calf, makes the protein particles in the milk clump together. Soon after she added the rennet water to the milk, whey (watery milk) appeared on top and curds (thick, custard-like clumps of protein) underneath. She cut the curds into small cubes, then stirred the curds and whey over a small fire. When the curds crumbled, she strained off the whey by pouring the mixture into a loosely woven basket lined with cheesecloth. Next, she mixed in some salt. The salted curds were stored in a cool place. Heavy weights (stones or bricks) were placed on top, and over many months the cheese was pressed until it became compact and solid. This was called curing the cheese.

Stir the curds and whey over the fire, then strain the mixture.

Add some salt.

Lift the curds from the basket.

Put weights on top and store in a dark place.

"Will you shear *my* lamb this year?" Sarah asked.

"Reckon so, she's plenty big enough now."

Out of the corner of her eye Sarah saw Meg's lips tighten. Meg had wanted the orphan lamb that Sarah fed by hand all last spring. But Pa had said no, it was Sarah's turn to start a little flock. Meg already had two sheep, and one was old enough to start lambing. She'd soon have more.

My turn, Sarah reminded herself contentedly, ignoring the angry clacking of her sister's knitting needles. A lamb of her own meant she was able to earn money, just like Mary Simpson. Knitted all the wool from her six sheep into thick boot socks, Mary had told them, and sold them for enough money to buy her bride clothes. Well, who needs those, Sarah thought, but having goods to trade when the pedlar came round, that would be something.

A few days after the sheep washing, Sarah and Willy were sent to round up the sheep. Their fleeces shone white in the sun, ready to be sheared.

Willy brought the new puppy, Nipper, along. "So he can learn to herd."

"Keep him away from here," Sarah warned, as the puppy yipped around her lamb, snapping at its heels until it bleated frantically.

Meg rescued Sarah's lamb and her own two and led them into the barn. Pa had swept the threshing floor clean for the shearing. George took hold of Sarah's lamb and held it down while Pa clipped, across the right shoulder, over the head and neck, down the left shoulder, under the belly. The fleece peeled off like bark from a birch tree. Sarah watched the sheep jump up and run bleating out of the barn. Poor thing, she thought, it's embarrassed, looking so skinny and bare.

Later that day, the sisters spread their fleeces out on the barn floor. Sarah watched intently as Meg began to snip away the dirty fringe that edged each fleece.

"It's not very big, that fleece of yours," Meg said after a few minutes of clipping. "What are you going to do with it?"

"Same as you. Knit mittens to trade."

"I've got a different plan this year," Meg announced. "I'm going to take mine to the weaver."

Sarah stared at her sister, impressed by her bold plan. Her own cloth. But why?

"And I'm not having any of Granny's homemade dyes, either," Meg stated grandly. "I'm buying cochineal from the store. I want a nice deep red." She gathered her clean fleece into a basket and flounced off, leaving Sarah full of speculations.

That evening, as the women sat in front of the cabin, teasing apart the curls of wool to get out the burrs and twigs, Meg said casually, "How much wool would it take for three yards of cloth, Granny?"

"Reach me your basket and I'll see what you've got." Granny lifted a handful of wool and weighed it in the palm of her hand. "That's good and thick. But you've only two fleeces. You'll mebbe need half a fleece as much again."

"Are you sure?" Meg sounded disappointed.

"Your granda, now, he could tell you to the ounce, but that would be my guess. Why do you need to know?"

Meg hesitated, then blurted out, "I want to take it to the weaver to make into a coverlet — for my hope chest."

Sarah was all ears. Surely Meg didn't need her hope chest filled so soon. True enough, Josh Turner had shown up once or twice in the winter and sat in embarrassed silence with them around the fire until George had asked him if he was moving in. "Rude little toad," Meg had hissed at her brother, but she hadn't seemed the least bit upset when Josh's visits stopped. There'd been other boys, hanging around at bees and frolics, but Meg had never seemed interested.

Ma looked up and frowned. "You've no need to be thinking of that just yet. You've got five good quilts put away and several towels and I don't know what else. You're doing very nicely. A woven coverlet can wait."

Meg picked fiercely at a burr snarling a handful of wool. "I want to do it this year," she muttered.

Meg always gets her own way, Sarah reflected, so she was only half surprised, several days later, when Meg made her a proposition. They were roaming through the fields, gathering wool. With such a small flock, the Robertsons couldn't afford to lose even a tuft of wool. So, baskets under

arms, the girls were picking fluff off bushes the sheep had brushed against.

"It's a shame to waste good wool, Sarah. Why don't you wait till you're better at spinning?"

Sarah felt nettled. Meg had been picking away at her the whole morning with comments about small fleeces and lumpy yarn.

"Pa said it was *my* turn. And Granny said I was good enough with the drop spindle that I could start using her wheel. So there, Margaret Robertson. You can just stop bullying me." The words popped out before she had time to think, but now that they were said, Sarah felt quite elated. She didn't often stand up to her big sister.

She skipped from bush to bush, picking fluff off twigs and tucking it into the walnut-sized opening in the top of her wool-gathering basket. As she worked she planned what she would do with her wool. With Granny and Meg using the spinning wheel she wouldn't get much chance to spin, but it didn't matter. She could spin a nice smooth thread on the drop spindle, no matter what Meg said. How many pairs of mittens could she have knitted up by the time the pedlar came?

"Sarah …" Meg's voice, soft and sweet, rang alarm bells in Sarah's head. She turned cautiously to look at her sister, who had been working beside her in angry silence for the past few minutes. "I really do need more wool for my coverlet."

I will not listen, Sarah told herself, turning away. She's not having her own way *this* time.

"Tell you what," Meg went on. "Let's do a trade. I'll spin your wool nice and fine in return for enough skeins to finish my coverlet."

"I already told you," Sarah said angrily, "there's nothing wrong with my spinning. I don't need you to do it."

They worked in a strained silence. Sarah's insides churned for several minutes. As she calmed down, a thought occurred to her. Maybe there *was* something she needed. She kept thinking about Mary Simpson and the boot socks. A pair of socks brought a lot more money than mittens. Both the store *and* the pedlar wanted socks. Well, why not? If she was old enough for her own sheep, she was old enough to move on from mittens.

"I'll tell you what I really want."

Meg turned an anxious face on her sister.

"I want to learn to turn a heel, a nice, strong, double heel the way you do. If you show me that, well … you can have your skeins."

"Done," said Meg quickly.

"*And,*" Sarah continued forcefully, "I don't want to be picked and pecked at all the time I'm learning."

Meg's face turned red. "Yes. All right," she muttered. She stood biting her lip and staring at Sarah. Now what? Sarah thought crossly, as Meg opened her mouth, drew in a breath and then hesitated.

"Sarah …" she said finally. "Sorry I said that … about your spinning."

CARDING AND SPINNING

Every pioneer family had a small flock of sheep. Producing wool was a necessity if the family was going to be warmly clothed through the long, cold winters.

Wool from the fleece is matted and tangled. Before it can be spun it has to be combed. This is called carding and is done with wooden paddles studded with wire teeth. A handful of matted wool is placed on one carder. Another carder is drawn across it, untangling the fibres in the same way you brush the tangles out of your hair. This action is repeated several times until the wool fibres line up with one another. To remove the wool, one carder is drawn backwards, making a roll of untangled wool called a sliver. The slivers are stored in a basket, waiting to be spun.

Spinning is simply pulling and twisting. Many fibres, including dog hairs and the absorbent cotton from a pill bottle, can be pulled and twisted to make a thread. But wool makes a particularly fine, strong thread. If you magnified a wool fibre, you'd see a series of overlapping scales. When the spinner twists the fibres, these scales interlock. The natural oil in wool, called lanolin, helps the fibres cling together.

carding

wool fibre
magnified
2000 times

a sliver
of wool

To make a smooth, strong thread, the spinner holds the sliver in one hand. With the thumb and forefinger of her other hand, she draws fibres out and twists them. As the twist travels up towards the handful of carded wool, more and more fibres feed into the thread. The experienced spinner knows just when to draw the thread out again to keep the wool from forming a lump, or slub.

A pioneer girl learned the rhythm of spinning by using a drop spindle, a stick about 20 cm (8 inches) long with a wooden disc at the end, acting as a weight. First she used finger spinning to make a short thread, which she fastened to the end of the spindle. She set the spindle spinning like a top while she drew out the wool fibres. This combination of twisting and drawing out made a fine, even thread. When the spindle reached the floor, the spinner wound the thread around the spindle and started again.

a drop spindle

Once a girl could use a drop spindle, she graduated to the walking wheel. Here, the spindle was attached to a large wheel that the spinner set in motion by pushing it with her hand or a stick. Then she walked back and forth.   As she walked away, the revolving wheel twisted the thread; as she walked back, the thread wound onto a bobbin. The bobbin, which was placed over the spindle, was often made from a dried corncob. A good day's spinning produced six skeins or 439 m (480 yards) of yarn, by which time the spinner had walked as many as 32 km (20 miles).

Scottish spinners often used a smaller wheel that allowed the spinner to sit down. The Scottish wheel had a foot treadle for turning the wheel and a removable wooden bobbin. Both these improvements made spinning faster and easier. This wheel could also be used to spin flax into linen thread.

As the bobbins filled with yarn they were laid in a basket until the spinner, or one of the children in the family, had time to wind the yarn onto the niddy noddy. Each turn around this frame measured 1.8 m (2 yards). Forty lengths around the niddy noddy made 73 m (80 yards), or one "knot" or "skein" of yarn. Skeins were measured carefully so the weaver would know exactly how much yarn he had to work with. Each skein of wool was twisted and looped one end through the other. This kept the yarn from knotting and tangling. It could be stored easily until it was time to dye it, weave it or knit it. As time went on, the hand-held niddy noddy was replaced by a winder, which had its own stand. Some winders even had counters that clacked loudly when 40 turns of wool had wound onto the frame.

niddy noddy unwound ...

... and wound

winder

SPINNING FLAX

Some families grew a grass-like plant called flax. After the stalks of this plant had been soaked and beaten, the fibres could be spun into a fine thread called linen and a coarse thread called tow. The spinner wet the flax with her fingers as she spun in order to mould the fibres into a twisted shape. Because she needed both hands to do this, she used a distaff, a stick with three upright projections, to hold the flax fibres.

From spinning come the words "distaff," to mean the female side of a family, and "spinster," to mean an unmarried woman. In olden times, spinning was considered a respectable way for an unmarried woman to earn a living.

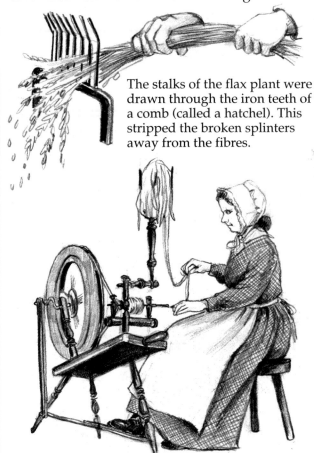

The stalks of the flax plant were drawn through the iron teeth of a comb (called a hatchel). This stripped the broken splinters away from the fibres.

Finger Spinning

You'll need:
- a small ball of absorbent cotton (ask for the cotton from the top of a pill bottle)

1. Hold the ball in your left hand, pinching one section loosely between your thumb and index finger.

2. With your right thumb and index finger, slowly pull out a few fibres. Twist as you pull. (If you are left-handed, hold the ball in your right hand and pull and twist with your left hand.)

What do you notice about the thread that forms?

- It should be strong. If it breaks easily you didn't twist for long enough.

- It should be smooth. If yours is lumpy you didn't pull steadily enough.

Pioneer spinners learned the rhythm needed to spin evenly. If they released the fibres steadily, the spinning wheel twisted them into a strong thread.

DYEING

Life in the backwoods was bleak and drab. To put a little colour into their lives, pioneer women dyed their wool before weaving it. The strongest colours came from store-bought dye — deep blue from indigo (a plant imported from the southern United States) or deep red from cochineal (obtained from a beetle and imported from Mexico). These expensive dyes were saved for special projects, such as bed coverlets. Fabric for clothing was dyed with herbal dyes.

All summer the women of the family hunted through the fields and woods for flowers, leaves and bark to dye their wool. Most wool was dyed with tea or crushed walnut shells to give a brown that wouldn't show the dirt. Chips from the logwood tree were used for a sombre black, for best wear and funerals. But the women also yearned for touches of brightness, so they gathered goldenrod blossoms or saved onion skins to make a soft yellow and looked for the flowers of Queen Anne's lace to make a soft green. Roots of the madder plant gave them a rusty red and blueberries, a faded blue.

The dyer needed 1 kg (2 pounds) of flower heads to dye 0.5 kg (1 pound) of wool. The blooms were boiled in water until the liquid became the desired shade. Then skeins of well-washed wool were simmered in the dye bath. Next, the dyer simmered the wool in a mordant to set the colour and keep it from fading or washing out. Today we use copperas and alum as mordants. The early settlers had to make do with urine. The acid in urine does a good job of making colours permanent.

Once coloured, the skeins of wool were stored in cedar baskets to keep them safe from moths.

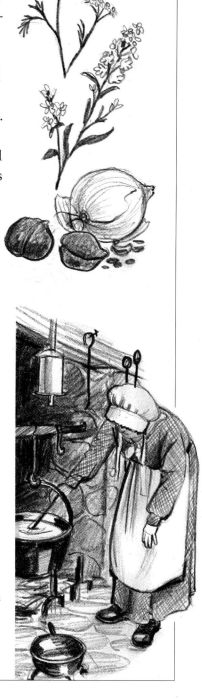

Onion-coloured Clothes

Early settlers learned how to use plants as dyes from the Native people and from their own experimentation. Here's how to dye a T-shirt yellow using onion skins.

You'll need:
- scissors
- 1 kg (2 pounds) dry outer skins from cooking onions
- 2 pots
- water
- 5 mL (1 teaspoon) alum (from a drugstore)
- 2 mL (½ teaspoon) washing soda (from a grocery store)
- a clean white T-shirt, clean handkerchief or clean scraps of cotton cloth
- a pair of rubber gloves
- a strainer

1. Use scissors to cut the onion skins into small pieces. Place them in a pot. Cover with water and let them soak overnight.

2. In another pot, mix the alum and washing soda with 4 L (1 gallon) of water. Soak your cloth in this overnight. The alum and washing soda create a mordant, which helps fix or bind the colour so that it won't run when you wash your cloth. Wear rubber gloves as you work, to prevent the mordant from drying your skin.

3. The next morning, simmer the onion and water mixture on medium heat for about an hour — ask an adult to help you. Strain out the onion skins and put them aside. Let the dye water cool.

4. Wearing rubber gloves, remove your cloth from the mordant and gently wring it out.

5. Place the cloth in the cooled dye water and add enough water to cover it. Simmer for 10 to 20 minutes. The longer you simmer the cloth, the deeper the colour will be. (The colour will be slightly lighter when the cloth is dry.)

6. Rinse your cloth in hot water and then cool water. Keep rinsing until the rinse water is clear. Hang your material to dry inside or in a shady place outside. (Sunlight will bleach natural dyes.)

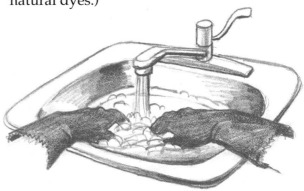

Follow the same instructions for dyeing with the plants listed below:

Plant		Colour produced
Coreopsis flowers		yellow
Lily of the valley leaves		pale green
Marigold flowers		brown
Dandelion leaves		yellow-green
Red hollyhock flowers		pink

WEAVING

One day in October Mr. Robertson saw a notice in the window of the general store:

WEAVING

JAMES MACRAE respectfully informs the Inhabitants of the district that he is prepared to WEAVE all kinds of PLAIN and FANCY

COVERLETS

in a workman-like manner and on reasonable terms, in Jamieson's Inn, for the next three months.

ORDERS NOW BEING TAKEN.

Meg's choice:
Four Snowballs pattern

The weaver set up his loom in the biggest room in the inn. Each day the women of the neighbourhood arrived with baskets full of yarn for the weaver to work with.

When Meg brought her white and red skeins of wool to the weaver, he showed her his pattern samples. She chose "Four Snowballs," a difficult pattern. Meg paid the weaver with extra skeins of wool. He used these to weave material to sell to the general stores.

In pioneer times, a good weaver could make 2.7 m (3 yards) of 76-cm (30-inch) wide cloth in a day. Few looms wove wider material as it was hard to throw a shuttle more than 76 cm (30 inches). By 1850, factories used a spring mechanism to shoot shuttles through the shed.

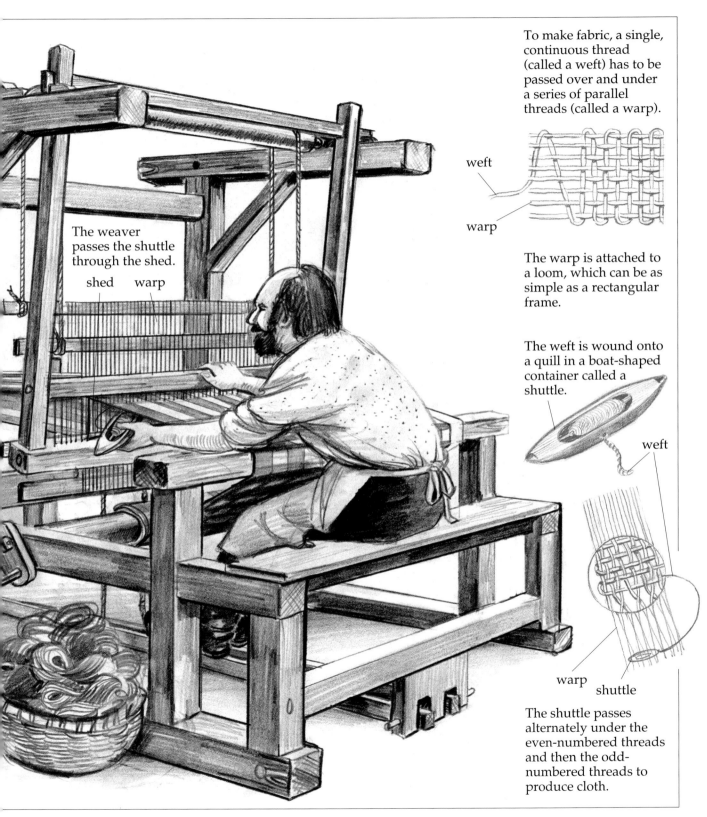

To make fabric, a single, continuous thread (called a weft) has to be passed over and under a series of parallel threads (called a warp).

weft

warp

The warp is attached to a loom, which can be as simple as a rectangular frame.

The weft is wound onto a quill in a boat-shaped container called a shuttle.

weft

The weaver passes the shuttle through the shed.

shed   warp

warp   shuttle

The shuttle passes alternately under the even-numbered threads and then the odd-numbered threads to produce cloth.

THE PEDLAR'S VISIT

Halloo, the house! Halloo-oo-oo, the house!" A musical jangle of pots and pans underlined the cry.

Sarah dropped the freshly washed diaper she had been spreading on the fence and ran. "The pedlar," she screeched. "The pedlar's coming!" As though everyone in the cabin wasn't already tumbling out the door. As though feet weren't pounding in from the near field.

"Call Pa and George," Ma said, wringing out the last of the washing. Meg, hands white with flour from baking, grabbed the dinner horn and blew with all her might. Willy arrived panting from the field where he'd been hoeing corn.

Only Granny sat unmoving, spinning away under the rowan tree. "All that noise!" she grumbled. "It'll not fetch him one whit faster!"

The man leading his horse up the path was Tobias Coombs, the same pedlar who had visited the Robertsons several times before. Any pedlar was welcome, but Tobias Coombs was special. He was — Sarah searched after the right words — almost a one-man circus or … or maybe a magician.

Willy had run down to meet the pedlar, and Sarah could hear her brother's high-pitched chattering as they walked up the path.

"My Jessy'd be much obliged to you for some water, young feller, me lad. Wait now, no need to fetch a bucket. Here's what she's used to." Tobias unfolded a large square of canvas and, with a few deft twists, refolded it into a pouch.

Willy made a dash for the river and the pedlar swept off his straw hat. "Mornin', Miz' Robertson, ma'am. Nice day to be out and about. Hope I see you all well."

Sarah could hardly wait until the greetings were over and the pedlar was sitting under the rowan tree with a mug of cider in his hands. What did he have in his packs? Would he take what she had to trade? Willy and George had several raccoon skins. Meg had a stack of knitted stockings. Are mine good enough? Sarah wondered about the three pairs of small stockings *she* had ready. Would Ma stop her from trading them? "You put a lot of work into those," Ma had said just last week, "so don't you waste them. Half a pedlar's goods are nothing but flash. You hold out for something you need."

"Well, here's my friend Lizzie," Tobias said, spotting the little girl peeking out from behind her mother's skirts. "If I had a piece of string I could show you such things … why, what d'you know? Here we are." He drew a length of string from his pocket and tied the ends.

Almost breathless with anticipation, Sarah pulled a stump stool over and settled down to watch. Willy sat cross-legged on the ground, all eyes. They'd seen this before, the cat's cradle games the pedlar wove in and out of his fingers, but every time they were mesmerized.

"I could do that," Willy always said, and Tobias would obligingly slip the circle of string over Willy's fingers. But of course Willy couldn't. The intricate web became a tangle of knots in Willy's hands, and the whole family laughed.

Sarah kept her eyes on Tobias. Now he was rooting about in a small sack at his feet. A pair of scissors and a square of black paper appeared. "Just turn sideways there, Sary-Sue," Tobias said to her. He always made up names for people. Last time she'd been Saratoga — a place he'd been to once, he said. "No, don't look at me. Turn your head." Sarah turned but kept darting looks sideways. What was he doing? She heard the snip of scissors and gasps from Ma and Meg.

"It's Sarah!" Lizzie squealed, and Sarah snapped her head around to see a perfect silhouette — chin, nose, eyes and fat braid down the back. A funny chill ran up her spine. *Is* that me? She'd only seen rippled images of herself in the river. A looking-glass was one of the things Meg was determined to get for their room in the new house.

"Paste that down on a piece of clean birch-bark and you'll have a nice picture for your wall."

Sarah was speechless with gratitude. She cradled the picture in her hands until the breeze lifted it like a kite.

"Mind you put it away safely," Ma said.

By the time Sarah had tucked the silhouette into the chest at the foot of her bed and run back out, Pa and George had arrived in from the fields. Tobias was spreading a blanket on the ground to set out the contents of his baskets.

"Oh, the markets and the trading ships were crammed with goodies this year. Now, I know you'll be needing these." He held out a palm full of nutmegs. Ma reached out and carefully chose one. "How are you for pins and needles, Meggie? And Master William, have you ever seen the like of this?" He held up a jackknife, its handle made of polished white bone. Just what Willy was hoping for, Sarah thought, as her brother held out his hand.

And so it went, through thimbles and buttons and lace and even two exquisitely painted tin boxes. Sarah looked with longing at everything, but each time Ma said firmly, "Not this time, thank you."

Tobias even teased Granny into trying on a pair of spectacles. "My eyes are as the good Lord made them," she sniffed. "No better and no worse." But Sarah noticed that before she gave the glasses back, Granny took a long look at the pattern she'd been knitting.

Pa sat smoking his pipe, watching with amusement as everyone got down to serious trading. "Higgling and haggling," Granny called it. The jackknife cost Willy both his raccoon skins. Meg talked Tobias out of a hairbrush for just one pair of her beautifully knitted stockings. Ma picked carefully through his stock, looking for necessities — one nutmeg, a paper of sewing pins, a tin dipper. "No fripperies," she said when Sarah pointed to the painted tin candle box. Sarah couldn't see anything else she wanted. The silhouette's enough, she decided.

The brisk swapping was winding down when the pedlar lifted one finger and said, "Now, the *pièce de résistance*, the prize of my collection." He held up a bundle swathed in a piece of old quilting. "Straight from Connecticut to you. No better like it anywhere. Pass it on to your grandchildren. Still be working like a dream."

With a flourish, he whipped off the cover to reveal a wooden clock. With a flick of his finger, he set the works going. A sturdy "tick tock" fell into the amazed silence.

Finally Pa cleared his throat. "Nice piece of work," he said slowly. "Good carving, I can see that, but —"

"The coming thing," Tobias interrupted. "Pretty soon everyone'll have 'em. Nice new house going up. Just the thing for your front parlour. Never have a problem timing your cakes again, ma'am." He turned a winning smile on Ma.

"Stuff and nonsense!" Granny snorted.

Sarah realized that Ma was sitting very still, staring at the clock. What a strange look, Sarah thought, like she's gone to sleep sitting up. Just then Ma gave a little shake of her head and said, in her usual brisk way, "Not this time, thank you. Come along in, girls, and we'll get the meal on the table. You'll stay to eat with us, Tobias?"

The pedlar looked up from repacking his baskets. "My pleasure, ma'am."

Through mouthfuls of fried pork, boiled potatoes and Meg's griddle cakes, Tobias told them all the news from up and down the countryside. He had them laughing so hard at his stories that everyone begged him to stay longer.

"Time and tide wait for no man," he said, wiping his mouth with the back of his hand. "Need to be on to the next place by sundown. Don't want my poor Jessy spooked by wolves or bears in them woods."

"I'll walk a piece with you," Pa said, and the two men set off with Jessy down the track to the forest trail.

Sarah was sitting under the rowan tree winding Granny's yarn onto the niddy noddy when Pa came back. She could see he was carrying something under his arm. Ma came out with the bowl of dishwater and threw it on the herb garden, then she stood watching as Pa approached. He held up the bundle, just the way the pedlar had, and whisked the cover away.

"I traded the lambskin," he said to Ma. "We said we'd use it for something special, remember?"

Sarah could tell by the way Ma was looking at Pa as she scrubbed her wet hands up and down her apron that she didn't mind about the lambskin. She didn't mind at all.

FROM BROKEN SOLES TO LOST SHEEP

All visitors were welcome on a backwoods farm. They brought news of the larger world, a break in the monotonous routine and stories of neighbours and town life. But perhaps the most exciting visitors were the wandering pedlars. To families who had to make everything from the trees they cut down, the animals they raised or hunted and the plants they grew, the pedlar's manufactured goods must have seemed like the riches of kings.

Because farms were few and far apart, pedlars went out to find customers instead of opening a shop in a village and expecting the customers to come to them. From spring to late fall, they travelled from farm to farm trading their goods or their services for whatever was available — sheepskins, ashes, furs, hog bristles, dried corn, even rags. Later, they sold these trade goods in large centres to make their money.

There were many different types of pedlars. Tobias Coombs was a "general pedlar," sometimes called a packman; he sold a variety of goods. But some pedlars offered only a few types of goods or a single service. Tinkers, for example, dealt only in tinware. They repaired pots and pans and sold new tin dippers and small pots.

Shoemakers were important pedlars. They sold and repaired shoes and boots, the hardest items of clothing to make at home. Some farmers could make clumpy, shapeless leather boots or had learned from the Native people how to make moccasins from rawhide, but most families went barefoot whenever possible to save shoe-leather. They waited for the cobbler or shoemaker to repair their old shoes on his yearly visit. What boots and shoes a family had were handed down until they wore out, so it was a great occasion when a child was old enough for a brand-new pair of boots.

The shoemaker was often a jack-of-all-trades. Besides making a family's shoes, he might cut their hair, sharpen their knives and saws, even pull aching teeth.

Even though most families made their own clothes, an itinerant tailor could make a good living by setting up for a few months in a community and offering to cut out the more difficult items, such as men's jackets and trousers. The women of the family would then sew them. If a young man was about to be married, he might have the tailor finish the suit as well. This would become his best suit, possibly for his entire life, stored carefully to preserve it from moths and worn only to weddings and funerals.

Native people travelled about the countryside trading various items they had made. The settlers were always glad to see Native women appear with baskets they had woven from split bark. In season, the Native people also traded blueberries or wild rice for flour.

Baskets and berries were the most common Native trade goods, but sometimes a family of Native people might arrive at a settler's door with maple sugar packed into mokuks (birchbark boxes), freshly caught fish or rabbit, tanned deerskin or a canoe. Settlers who were new to the bush were particularly happy to see the Native traders. With all the hard work, their European clothing wore out quickly, and they depended on the Native people for deerskin to make new trousers and skirts until they had enough sheep to provide wool for cloth.

THE SHOEMAKER AT WORK

The shoemaker sat on one end of a special cobbler's bench.

Lasts (wooden forms carved in the shape of a foot) were used to shape the upper part of the boot. These shaped uppers were then stitched or pegged to the soles. The same last was used for both feet, and the new owner switched boots from right foot to left to make them wear evenly.

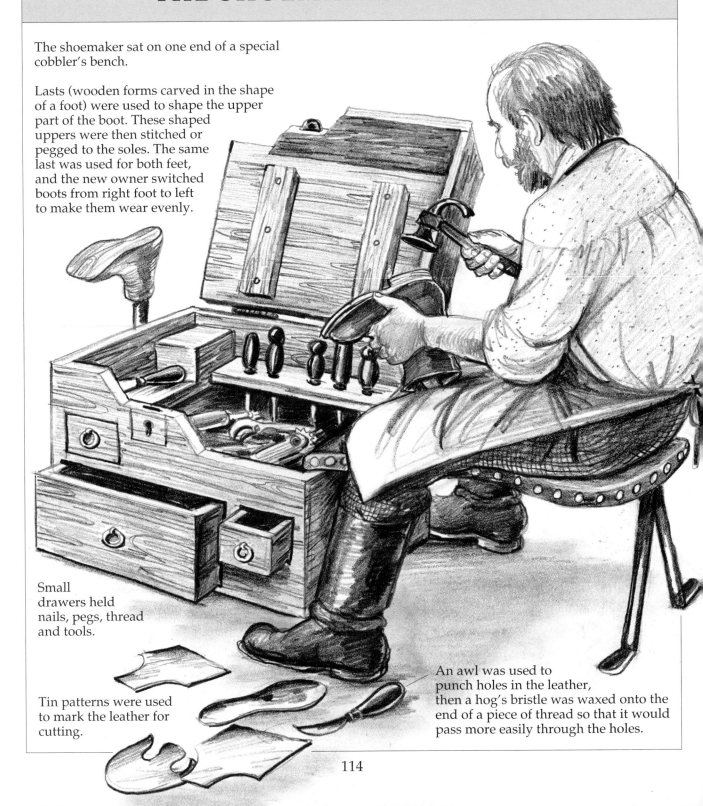

Small drawers held nails, pegs, thread and tools.

Tin patterns were used to mark the leather for cutting.

An awl was used to punch holes in the leather, then a hog's bristle was waxed onto the end of a piece of thread so that it would pass more easily through the holes.

THE ITINERANT PREACHER

I'm hunting for lost sheep in the wilderness," said the man on horseback.

"I'm sorry, sir," Willy replied politely. He tipped his head back to take a closer look, but the broad-brimmed hat hid the traveller's face. "I'm afraid the wolves will have them by now. We keep our sheep penned up."

"Take me to your parents, boy," the man said with a hint of a smile. "They'll know the kind of sheep I'm after."

This was Willy's first meeting with the saddlebag preacher, but it wasn't his last. Twice a year, from that day on, Jabez Jones arrived at their farm with his Bible in one saddlebag and his fiddle in the other. George and Willy were sent running to invite all the neighbours to the schoolhouse. There Jabez preached and played hymns while the gathering sang heartily, almost as though they were trying to sing away all the frustrations of the past year.

Most backwoods families lived too far from the nearest town to attend church services, so they looked forward to visits from the preacher. Many of these men covered 320 to 480 km (200 to 300 miles) a month, slogging along muddy trails or getting lost in the forest, eaten by insects in summer and trapped by storms in winter. They were made welcome by people starved for spiritual comfort to lighten their work-weary days. In summer, when a preacher was expected, the neighbourhood sometimes organized a camp meeting. People came from great distances to take part in the singing and preaching.

THE TINKER

Each time the tinker visited, Mrs. Robertson had a good look at the tinware he carried. Tin plate was lightweight and could be formed easily into such articles as mugs, dippers, candlesticks, lanterns, mouse-proof boxes, cookie cutters and reflector ovens. It was a great improvement over heavy wooden ware and drab pewter.

Because of its shiny surface, tin plate was called "poor man's silver." If the surface was scratched or pitted, it soon rusted. To stop this from happening, tinsmiths coated the tin with a tar-based shellac that turned the silvery metal black. Then they used bright colours to paint on flowers and other designs.

Punched-hole designs were also used to decorate tinware, especially lanterns. The holes let the light from a candle inside shine through.

Make a Punched-tin Picture

You'll need:
- paper
- a pencil
- tape
- an aluminum foil pie plate
- heavy cardboard
- a nail and hammer

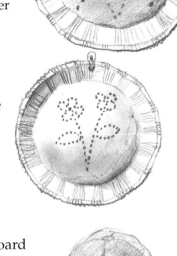

1. Draw a simple design on the paper with the pencil. Here are some ideas to get you started.

2. Tape the paper to the pie plate.

3. Place the cardboard on the tabletop to protect the surface as you hammer. Gently hammer the nail in at even intervals along the outline of the design.

116

Make a Pioneer Water Carrier

Tobias Coombs had enough to carry without adding a heavy water bucket to his load. But both he and his horse needed water, and it wasn't always possible to wade into a stream and drink. His solution was a square of canvas; it was easy to carry and easy to fold into a watertight pouch as big as a bucket.

Here's how he folded his pouch. Why not try folding a smaller version in paper to make a drinking cup for yourself?

4. To hang, punch a hole in the top of the rim.

5. To make a candle shield, cut straight across the bottom of the pie plate and bend the plate into a curve. Stand this up in front of a lit candle in a candle-holder. Pioneers often used shields (called sconces) to keep the candle from blowing out or to protect the wall from the smoke and heat.

1. Fold a square of paper in half on the diagonal.

2. Fold the sides in.

3. Fold one flap down and tape it.

4. Pioneers would have used the top flap as a handle, but you can tape it down on the other side.

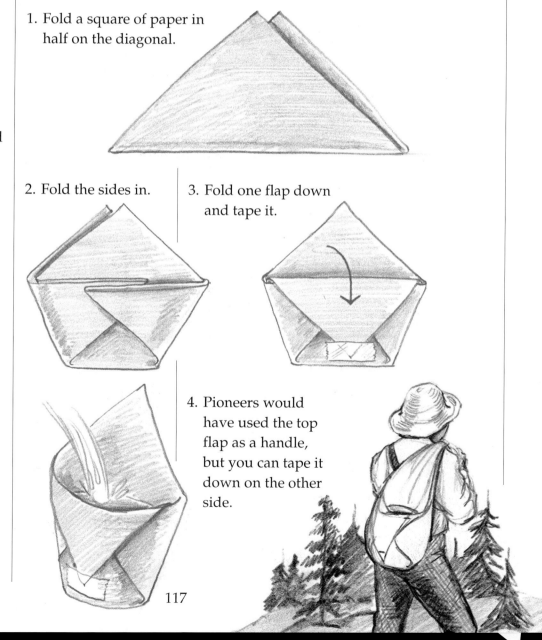

117

KEEPING TIME

The Robertsons didn't need to know when it was exactly ten o'clock in the morning or five o'clock at night. There were no television shows to keep track of or swimming lessons to be on time for. They got up with the sun and went to bed shortly after the sun set. If they slept in, the rooster's crowing woke them. But they *did* need to know when it was noon so they could have dinner halfway through the day. And Mrs. Robertson and the girls needed some way of measuring time when they were cooking.

How did they measure time? The sun helped. Anyone who works out of doors learns to mark the sun's passage across the sky. For example, when the sun is overhead, it is midday, or noon.

Shadows helped, too. Most settlers made primitive sundials. A stick was set up so that it cast a shadow over a series of marks as the sun moved across the sky. The simplest "shadow clock" was a line cut in a carefully chosen place in the floor of the cabin. The sun's rays, shining through a crack in the door, would cast a shadow along this line at noon. A slightly more elaborate version of this could be made by cutting marks along a windowsill. On cloudy days, the farmwife would simply have to guess the time.

To measure short periods — the baking time for bread or pies, for example — marks were cut in the sides of candles. Experienced cooks knew that when a candle had burned down a few centimetres (an inch or two), it was time to take the bread out of the oven. A slightly more accurate timer could be made by filling a paper or birch-bark cone with sand and wedging it in a jar. The cook knew how much sand had to run through the tiny hole in the point of the cone to mark the baking time of her pies or cookies. These "sand clocks" were also used by preachers to time their sermons. Well-to-do people had hourglasses containing sand, which could be turned over and reset when the sand had run through.

These timers were not all that accurate, but they were the best people could do until pedlars arrived with clocks. Some pedlars carried just the inner workings, leaving the new owner to make a case for the clock; others carried the finished product, often with a beautifully carved case. Two popular styles were the Connecticut clock and the steeple clock.

Even though these clocks had cogs and wheels carved from wood, rather than made from steel, they were remarkably accurate and long-lasting. Many can be found today, ticking away the hours in museums and pioneer villages.

Make a Sand Clock

You'll need:
- 2 small plastic wine glasses (with hollow stems)
- white glue
- a metal barbecue skewer
- scissors
- candle and match
- plastic wrap
- a rubber band
- sticky tape
- enough sand to fill one glass

1. Glue together the stems of the glasses.

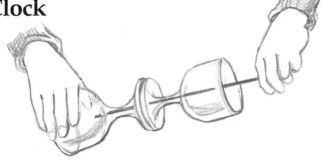

2. Ask an adult to help you with this next step. Use a skewer heated over a candle to poke a hole through the stems, from one glass to the other. Work carefully and slowly so you don't crack the plastic.

3. Cut a piece of plastic wrap double the size needed to fit over the mouth of one of the glasses. Hold it in place with a rubber band while you wind the tape around it.

4. Pour sand into the second glass. Fill or half fill it, depending on how much time you want the clock to measure. Tape another doubled piece of plastic wrap over the mouth of the sand-filled glass.

5. Turn your clock so that the sand is on top and set it on a tabletop. Use a clock (or a watch that indicates seconds) to measure the amount of time the sand takes to run from one glass to the other. Your sand clock will measure only that amount of time. Many people use this type of clock to time boiling eggs.

Perfect 3-minute eggs!!

119

FISHING

Willy dog-paddled to the river bank and scrambled up on a rock to dry. He felt proud of himself. For the first time he'd managed to stay beside Nekeek right across the swimming hole and partway back. He watched Nekeek streak across again. Just like an otter, he thought. Nekeek said otters were his brothers because that's what his name meant.

Life had been a lot more interesting since he'd met Nekeek. Willy remembered the day four dark, silent men had appeared in the farmyard. He had ducked behind the oxen, too scared to stand beside his father. Then he'd noticed a boy.

The boy stared around the yard, then walked right towards Willy's hiding place. "How'd you know I was here?" Willy stammered. The boy smiled and pointed to Willy's bare feet, visible below the hairy bellies of the oxen. Then he drew a large hunting knife from its buckskin sheath and held it out.

Willy's heart stopped pounding as he admired the bone-handled knife. "Like to see mine?" He pulled his new jackknife from his pocket. The Indian boy turned it over and over on his palm, obviously puzzled. "Like this." Willy swung the blade out until it clicked, and the boy laughed. From that moment they were fast friends.

The boys didn't see each other every day. But about once a week, without warning, Nekeek would appear at the door and off they would go exploring. Willy hadn't yet visited the Indian camp down the river. He was still nervous of Nekeek's father and uncles, who had come to ask Pa's permission to camp on his land. Every so often, one of the uncles would appear with a large fish or a brace of rabbits, and Ma would give him some flour or salt in exchange.

A cool breeze made Willy shiver. He reached for his shirt to dry himself. By the time he'd shrugged into his wool breeches, Nekeek was back and pulling on buckskin leggings. Why can't I wear clothes like that? Willy thought, tugging at the wool scratching his still-damp legs.

Suddenly Nekeek said, "Uncle," and nodded his head at the trees behind Willy.

Willy spun around. Almost close enough to touch stood one of the dark, silent men. Nekeek fell in behind his uncle, and they moved off in single file along the river bank. Willy stared after them, disappointment knotting his stomach, until he heard Nekeek's "Come." In a flash, he was pounding after them.

"Where we going?" he panted as he fell in line behind Nekeek. His friend just shrugged and glided silently after his uncle. Willy heard himself crunching and crashing along the trail. Like a wild boar, he thought. Why can't I walk like them? He was hot and sticky by the time they finally stopped. The river ran shallow here, quiet and overhung with leafy branches. The uncle waded into a shade-dappled pool. Nekeek hunkered down on the bank and Willy hunched down beside him. "What ..." he started to ask, but Nekeek held up his hand.

The uncle stood motionless, bending from the waist, his arms hanging down in front of him, wrist-deep in the water. The boys watched and watched. Nothing happened. Willy heard a fly buzzing, then felt it alight on the back of his neck. It walked down his spine, tickling, tickling. Willy twitched a muscle. The fly walked on. Just as Willy thought he couldn't bear another second, the uncle moved. With a scoop and a flick of one hand, he sent a good-sized trout flying onto shore. He stalked over, knocked its head against a rock and dropped it into a basket tied to his waist. Then he pointed at Nekeek.

As his friend waded into the stream, Willy had a horrible thought. What if he points at me next? Sweat broke out on his forehead. I can't fish that way. Suddenly he heard Nekeek's hand slap the water. No fish landed on the bank. The uncle stared stonily at his nephew. Nekeek hunched over the water again. This time he let his hands dangle right in the water.

Willy took a deep breath. Maybe Nekeek can't do it, either. Maybe he's still learning. He watched carefully. Bend over, hands in water, keep very still, scoop out. Like a bear does it. Maybe I *can*. Just then Nekeek flipped a fish onto the bank. He knocked its head against a rock and handed it to his uncle.

Why doesn't he cheer or something? Willy wondered. Then he realized they were both looking at him. He swallowed. "Sure. Sure — I'll try." His voice sounded too loud, even with the gurgle of the water over rocks.

Why not? Can't be that difficult, he told himself as he waded into the stream. He bent over, just as the others had done. Arms straight, hands in water, don't move. He stared beyond the dappled surface. There. A fish. He snatched and his hand closed on water. A shadow. Nothing but the shadow of a falling leaf. Ignoring the two watchers on the bank, he concentrated on the water. Shadows flicked from side to side. He wanted something darker, moving forward. There! But it was gone faster than his thought. Be patient. Be patient. It only took Nekeek a few minutes. His back was aching. What if he straightened? A dark shadow flashed past. Better stay still. He tried to quiet his breathing, calm the twitch of an arm muscle. At the slightest motion, the slow-moving fish darted away. Then he saw a shadow near the bottom, flicking a lazy tail, inching forward. Now! He scooped and flipped. To his amazement, onto the bank flopped a small trout.

"I did it!" he shouted. The uncle grunted. Nekeek stunned the fish with a rock, then wrapped it in leaves and handed it gravely to Willy. With a jerk of his head, he indicated his uncle, already disappearing into the forest. Willy fell in line behind them. He didn't even try to stop the grin that lit up his face.

As he came through the front field he saw his mother and grandmother sitting on the front porch shelling peas. George was carrying a bucket of water towards the house. "Look, George! Caught a trout for dinner."

"Pretty puny excuse for a fish," George jeered, swinging his bucket of water onto the porch. Willy didn't care. Wait till ol' George heard how he caught it!

Granny reached out for the leaf-wrapped trout. "There's a clever lad. How did ye manage that, now?"

"Nekeek's uncle showed me. You stand really still with your hands in the water till the fish comes by, then you just scoop it out."

"You liar!" George shouted. "No one can catch a fish that way."

But Granny was laughing. "Och, aye! Tickling trout. Your granda was a dab hand at that. Many's the poached fish we had from the laird's stream. Scooped up just that way. Good for you, young Will!"

WILD FOOD

Salt pork and more salt pork — the early settlers' diets were boring and unhealthy unless the family could take time from the endless clearing and planting and get out into the woods and streams to hunt and fish.

Fishing took the least skill and equipment. The children were often sent off to catch sunfish and perch with little more than a piece of twine and some fatty bacon for bait. The mother would take a basketful of these little fish, add parsley, thyme and onion and boil it all up into a tasty soup.

Older boys and men often went night fishing for larger fish and eels. For this they needed pronged spears and a jack light. This was made of strips of iron shaped into a basket and attached to a pole. Pine knots sticky with resin were piled into the basket and set on fire. The fishermen waded into the stream, then stood quietly waiting for the light to attract the fish. On a lake, night fishing was done from a large canoe with the jack light lashed to the prow (front). Spearing and netting big fish such as pike, pickerel and muskellunge was wet work.

The Robertsons looked forward to having deer meat (called venison) as a welcome change from salt pork. Mr. Robertson didn't waste time stalking deer. If he spotted a deer making a regular visit to the stream or a salt-lick, he would lie in wait for it. His musket had only a short range, so he had to get very close to hit the deer. Often the deer would only be wounded, and Mr. Robertson would follow it until it fell. Then the boys helped him drag the carcass through the woods on a sledge.

Some animals were dangerous pests. Raccoons could destroy a whole field of corn in one night, so the Robertsons were always on the watch for them. Once or twice every summer, Mr. Robertson joined the neighbours in a raccoon hunt. Willy and George stretched and dried the skins, which would be traded at the store or made into caps or sleigh blankets. The fat was boiled down to use for cooking or in oil lamps.

Sheep were often attacked by bears and wolves. Hunting them was dangerous, but if the flocks were threatened, the neighbours would band together on a hunt.

Sometimes Mr. Robertson and George went squirrel hunting. The fur made warm linings for cloaks, and the meat made a tasty stew.

GUNS

Hunters need guns. Guns need bullets (or shot) and gunpowder. All of these were expensive and hard to come by in the backwoods. The Robertsons, like most backwoods farmers, had an old percussion musket. Mr. Robertson bought gunpowder and a bar of lead at the general store. On winter nights he melted down the lead in an iron ladle and poured it into a mould to make round lead bullets called musket balls.

The gunpowder was put in a powder horn (made from a cow's horn). The musket balls were kept in a leather pouch. To load the gun a hunter poured a small amount of powder down the barrel, dropped in a small square of linen and rammed both down with a rod. After this he dropped in the bullet and rammed another linen square down tightly on top of the ball. Finally he was ready to shoot.

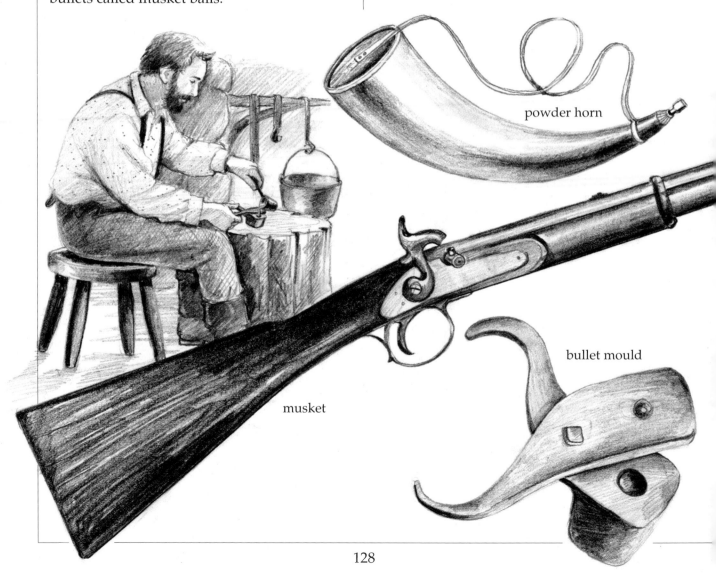

powder horn

musket

bullet mould

When he pulled the trigger, a small hammer hit a copper cap, making a spark that ignited the gunpowder. The exploding gunpowder propelled the bullet out of the gun barrel. If the gun wasn't loaded properly, it could burst, causing a serious accident.

George practised shooting at a log set up as a target. When he finished he had to pry out the bullets with his knife and set them aside to be recast into new bullets. Lead was too expensive to waste.

NETTING OR SNARING

Not all hunting was done with a gun. Passenger pigeons were often caught in nets. In the fall, when large flocks were migrating, they landed to feed among the stubble of freshly cut wheat fields. Some farmers stretched nets between two upright poles, to catch the birds as they landed; others made a trap in which a net propped up by a stick fell on the birds. Sometimes the birds were so plentiful they could be knocked out of the trees with sticks.

Pigeons, roasted or baked in pies, were a treat, and the early settlers killed and salted down thousands each year. Gradually the huge flocks grew smaller until, on March 24, 1900, the last passenger pigeon was shot and the birds became extinct.

Other wild birds, such as geese, partridge and wild turkeys, and small animals, especially hares, were also hunted or snared.

NATIVE HUNTERS

Once or twice a year, Native hunters arrived at the door. Mr. and Mrs. Robertson were always glad to see them. Their visit meant venison, rabbit, wild partridge or fish to trade for flour or potatoes. Mrs. Robertson and Granny also wanted to learn from the women about woodland plants that made good medicines.

Willy felt nervous on his first visit to Nekeek's summer camp, but he soon felt as much at home there as in his own front yard.

Nekeek's family travels with two other families. At each camp, the families set up huts made of poles covered with bark. Poles are cut at each camp, but the bark is rolled carefully by the women and carried with them.

Otter skins are stretched over hoops of willow branches to dry. Every day Nekeek's uncles and cousins go off in their canoes to hunt otter. Nekeek wishes he was old enough to go.

Nekeek's mother and aunts prepare ash wood and weave it into baskets.

A stew of otter or beaver meat bubbles all day. To get the iron pot, Nekeek' mother traded dried otte skins at the store.

The baby sleeps on her cradleboard. Instead of a diaper, moss is packed into the leather bag to keep her dry.

Nekeek's sisters search the forest for tasty roots, mushrooms and plants to add to the stew pot. In the fall they harvest wild rice from the shallow parts of lakes.

Nekeek and Willy play knuckle-bones (a form of jacks).

Fishwatcher's Guide

Nekeek's family and the Robertsons learned the ways of fish because they needed fish for food. You don't have to catch your dinner, but you can still enjoy watching fish.

- Walk softly. Sound travels through rock and soil into water. Loud footsteps will scare away the fish.

- Try to keep the sun at your back. This reduces the glare off the water and lets you see clearly under the water. But don't let your shadow move over the water. This will alert the fish.

- Sometimes you can't get away from the glare. If all you can see is a reflection of your face, blink, then stare beyond the reflection. Soon, underwater shapes should come into focus.

- Get as high as possible above the water. Looking down from a bridge gives you a wonderful view of the bottom of a river.

- Fish see the world differently than you do. Rays of light passing through water are bent (or refracted). Because of this, a fish looking up can also see what's off to the side — almost as though it was looking through a periscope. For this reason, a fish will see you approaching if you walk upright. Crouch as you near the shore, or the fish will be long gone before you reach the water.

- Fish are usually found where food is plentiful or where there's shade and protection. In lakes and ponds, look under piers and docks, in weed beds or around the edges of lily pads. Good spots in rivers and streams are near dams and falls (where deep holes provide protection), behind big rocks and under overhanging brush or trees.

132

Playing Knuckle-bones

Nekeek and his family moved from place to place and had to carry their belongings with them. Knuckle-bones was the ideal game for them. They only needed some leftover bones — no need to transport cumbersome materials.

Games similar to knuckle-bones have been played by people all over the world. The tosses and catches of the game take both skill and luck. As a result, knuckle-bones sometimes involved gambling or predicting the future.

You'll need:
- 2 to 4 players
- 5 neck bones from a turkey or chicken (stones, nuts or buttons can also be used)
- a small space

1. Each player takes a turn. A player throws down the bones and picks one up. This is called the jack. The player tosses the jack in the air, then, with the same hand, picks one bone off the ground and catches the jack before it falls.

2. The player puts the picked-up bone in his or her free hand and tosses the jack again. He or she continues until all four bones have been picked up. If a player drops the bones, misses the jack or moves another bone, he or she is out, and the next player gets a turn.

3. After a player has successfully picked up all four bones, he or she tries to pick up two bones at a time and repeats this until all have been picked up. Repeat the pattern, picking up four bones at a time.

4. Make the game more interesting by inventing complicated patterns. For example, a pattern called stables is played like this: Throw down the bones. Place one hand on the ground with fingers apart. Toss the jack, flick a bone into the "stable" formed by two parted fingers, then catch the jack. Repeat this until all four bones are in four different stables.

133

HARVESTING THE CROPS

"Stand up properly," Meg said. "You can't carry water all hunched over like that."

Willy wiggled his shoulders to make the yoke sit more comfortably, then straightened up. The weight of the buckets made the wood bite into the back of his neck.

"It hurts," he complained.

"Stop fidgeting." Meg moved the yoke slightly and the pressure eased. "You'll be fine. It's a lot easier than lugging a bucket by hand. And you won't lose nearly so much water. Off you go. The men will be dying of thirst."

Carrying water out to the hayfield had always been Meg's or George's job. This year Pa wanted George's help with the harvesting, and Ma had decided that Willy and Sarah were big enough to carry water.

Stupid buckets, Willy grumbled to himself as he trudged off, I want to do real work. Like George. That reminded him of George sitting at the grindstone last evening. Making *me* turn the handle while he sharpened the sickle. Thinks he's so important just because Pa's letting him help cut the hay this year.

The sun beat down from a blue sky. Pa had been right about the weather. "Listen to those cicadas sing," he'd said the night before. "We'll have good haying weather tomorrow."

Willy rested his hands on the bucket handles to keep them from swinging and arched his back against the weight. Across the fields he could see Pa and one of the big Simpson boys who'd been hired on for the summer. They swayed back and forth as they swung the long-handled scythes to cut the hay. George was bent over using the short-handled sickle to trim around a tree stump. Every so often Pa stopped and ran a whetstone over his scythe blade. Willy liked the raspy *zzzzrooop* of the whetstone sharpening the blade.

The stubble of cut grass prickled Willy's bare feet as he crossed the field. The soles of his feet were toughened from months of running barefoot, but with the buckets dragging him down, the stubble felt sharp. And he was anxious about tripping over an upthrust stone and spilling the water or, worse still, stepping on a snake. With luck, the snakes would all be gone. Just yesterday he and George had been out with sticks beating the field to scare away snakes and families of skunks and rabbits. "Last thing I want," Pa had said, "is animals exploding out of the grass in front of me when I'm swinging a scythe. Like to cut a foot off."

"Ah! Here he is." Pa straightened and stretched. "Time for a rest, boys." Willy lowered the buckets carefully to the uneven ground, shrugged off the yoke and handed around the gourds he'd brought as water dippers.

"Now that you're here," Pa said, "you can stay a while and spread some of that hay. Can't spare anyone from the cutting till we're farther along."

George smirked, licked a finger and flicked it across the sharp edge of the sickle as though to say, I'm indispensable. *You* can do the baby work. Willy waited till Pa's back was turned, then stuck out his tongue at George. It wasn't much but it made him feel a little better. In the afternoon, Ma and the girls came out to help. Finally, at the end of a long hot day, Pa said, "Well, we've done our best. Let's hope the sun does its best."

For two days the sun baked and dried the hay. On the third morning, the whole family turned out to rake it into wind-rows to make loading the sledge easier. Up and down the fields they went, competing with one another to make straight, even rows. "A thing worth doing is worth doing well," Ma always said. Several times during the morning, Willy or Sarah went back to the house to get buckets of cool water to which Granny had added a handful of oatmeal to make a thirst-quenching drink. As Willy trudged out once more with the water buckets, he looked up at the sky. Clouds like balls of carded wool were rolling in. But they were high and white. No danger from rain there.

After the noon meal Pa walked the oxen and sledge out to the field. Pitching hay onto the sledge was hard work for Willy. His arms weren't strong enough to throw a forkful to the top of the load. More often than not his stalks slithered off. Finally, Pa, who was up on top building the load, said, "Willy, you take charge of the oxen. Keep moving them forward as we work along this row."

The afternoon dragged on. One load was safely back at the barn with another still to come. Ma and Meg were pitching hay now while Sarah carted water. Back at the barn, Pa and George were starting to build the haystack.

Hour after hour, Willy inched the oxen along the rows, watching out for stones and roots and stumps. In between times, he scanned the sky. The woolly clouds bunched and drifted into fantastic shapes, and Willy's mind drifted with them. A bear and her cub lumbered across the sky, a dainty pony skipped by, then fat fish blowing bubbles, a grey whale. Grey? "Ma, look! Rain clouds."

Ma took one quick look at the sky and said, "Get those oxen moving, Willy. We've got to get this load under cover."

"Heyup," Willy shouted, and the oxen started a steady plod. Low clouds scudded in, darker with each second. Ma and Meg frantically raked wind-rows into small haycocks. In piles, at least the bottommost stalks would stay dry. Willy concentrated on the sledge. "Gee, Buck, gee, Bright," he shouted to steer the oxen around roots and stumps. As the sky grew darker, he prodded the animals with the goad. "Move, move," he urged them. The oxen blew through their nostrils and plodded steadily ahead. "Never was such a stubborn beast as an ox," his father always said.

Willy could see Pa and George beside the barn. They swung their arms in rhythm, oblivious to everything but the orderly layering of the haystack. Then he felt a drop of water.

"Pa," he screeched. "Rain, rain!" The sudden noise started Bright off at a trot, with his partner snorting beside him. Pa and George wrenched open the big barn doors and, just as the clouds burst, the sledge skidded under cover.

"Good work, Willy," Pa said as they all crowded into the barn. "You saved that load. You've got a real farmer's eye for weather."

Willy glowed with pride. For the next few days, as he worked, he pictured over and over his mad dash for the barn until it grew into a story of heroic proportions. When Uncle Jacob Burkholder came over to show Pa how to thatch a waterproof roof for their haystack, Willy regaled him with the whole tale.

"Well now, that's quite a feat — moving cattle beasts along like that. Mind you, nothing like a drop of rain to get a man moving." Uncle Jacob laughed as he wove the last of the straw into the roof. "Now I remember when I was a young'un, no older'n you, we saw a dilly of a storm heading up. My brother and I were running around fastening shutters and bolting doors when we heard a tarnation big racket headed our way. Up our lane come a farm rig, horses running like Jehu, all wild-eyed and foaming at the mouth. Wagon bouncing along behind like a pea on a hot skillet. 'Runaway,' my brother shouts. Then we see the driver's whipping them horses and screaming, 'Open the doors. Open the doors!' We jumped pretty smart, I can tell you. Swung open those big barn doors, and he drove the whole rig in just seconds before a great crack of thunder. And did those clouds pour rain! I looks in the wagon and sees three hundredweight of flour in linen sacks. A few drops of rain and the whole lot would've caked solid. That man never was any good at reading the weather," Uncle Jacob ended scornfully. "Well, there's your stack roofed in. No fear of rain getting through that."

Ma had been busy, too. While she was listening to Uncle Jacob's story she'd bound a handful of hay into the shape of a rooster. "Here, Willy," she said, "scoot up and stick that on top. It'll dress up the stack for us."

"Good idea," beamed Uncle Jacob. "And I'll show you how to rig it up as a weather-vane so's you'll be warned the next time a storm blows up."

HARVESTING

The hot days of summer brought hard work for the whole family.

The Robertsons had two hayfields. One they had cleared themselves. The other was a beaver meadow. Long before the Robertsons arrived on the land, beavers had dammed the river and flooded several hectares (acres). The trees died, the water dried up and grass grew. Early settlers were delighted to find beaver meadows on their farms because they provided instant fodder (food) for oxen and cows.

The hay would feed the animals through the winter, but the people needed wheat. In fact the wheat harvested one autumn had to last until the next. By the first week of August, the wheat was ready to be cut. The men were out in the fields with their scythes again, and Willy and Sarah were running back and forth with water.

As the men cut the wheat, Mrs. Robertson and Meg followed behind tying the stalks of grain into bundles called sheaves. Ten sheaves propped up against one another formed a stook.

Wheat was a precious crop, and the family worked long into the night to get it safely under cover. Mr. Robertson and the hired help packed it carefully into mows (storage lofts) in the barn to keep it safe and dry until they had time to thresh it.

Harvesting wasn't all hard work. Sometimes neighbours helped one another bring in the crops. This harvesting bee often finished with a party. The men set up long tables in the fields, and the women brought out food for a harvest supper. To amuse the children, Mr. Burkholder built a maze out of sheaves of grain.

HARVEST MOON

Farmers planned to harvest when the moon was full, so that they had enough light to work until midnight if necessary. In September, the full moon seems to linger in the sky for several nights in a row. This happens because moonrise comes only 20 minutes later each night, instead of the usual 50 minutes. No wonder the September full moon was called the harvest moon.

Full moons were useful all year round. Many farmers believed that crops planted at certain phases of the moon would grow better. To escape the heat of the day, planting and hoeing were often done in the cool of the night by the light of the moon. In winter, travellers going on long journeys planned their trips for when the full moon would give them extra light to get home through the dark forest.

Reading the Weather

Thanks to the weather forecasts, you can make plans, not just for tomorrow but for the whole week. Pioneers didn't have trained meteorologists reporting by radio or television. They predicted good and bad weather by watching for signals in the world around them. Try the pioneer method of forecasting the weather.

Good weather signs are: birds flying high, smoke rising quickly, cicadas singing loudly and heavy dew at night. Watch the clouds. The higher they are, the better the weather will be.

These signs mean wet weather's coming: smoke curling downward, dark cumulus (or cotton-ball) clouds, overcast cirrus (or long, stringy) clouds. A halo around the sun means rain within 10 to 12 hours.

THRESHING

A good wheat harvest meant the family would have flour for the coming year. But there were many steps between fetching in the grain and having flour for baking bread.

First, the grain seeds had to be separated from the stalks. To do this, the farmer spread several bundles of wheat on the wooden floor in the centre of the barn. Then he and his helpers beat the heads of the wheat with a flail, a tool made from two sticks joined together with a length of chain or a leather hinge. As the thresher swung the handle, the flail whipped down and pounded the wheat heads, shaking the seeds, or kernels, free.

threshing

Soon kernels and husks, or chaff, lay in heaps on the floor. To separate the good part of the wheat, the kernels, from the useless part, or chaff, the farmer needed a winnowing tray. In the early days this was simply a sheepskin tacked to a wooden hoop. Later, the tray was made from wood or tin. On a windy day, the farmer and his helper shovelled the mixture of kernels and chaff into the tray, then shook it up and down. The light chaff was lifted by the wind and blown away. The grain could also be winnowed by pouring it from a height, so that the heavy grain fell onto a clean sheet spread on the ground, while the light chaff blew away. Winnowing was hard, dirty work, and farmers worked constantly to improve their tools and techniques for sifting out the chaff.

By the end of the day everyone in the barn was choking on dust, but the family had eight linen sacks full of grain and a mow crammed with straw (the leftover stalks from the wheat) to use as bedding for the animals. Now they were ready to haul the precious sacks of cleaned grain to the grist mill.

winnowing

142

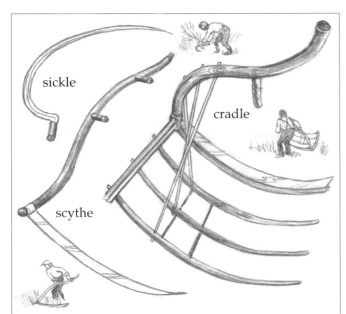

sickle

cradle

scythe

SICKLES & SCYTHES

Farms today have smooth, rolling fields. Tractors and threshing machines can move over these fields easily, harvesting the crops quickly. Pioneer fields were rough and uneven, dotted with tree stumps and covered with stones. To cut down the crop, the harvester would grab a handful of stalks, cut it with a short-handled sickle and lay it on the ground. This meant hours of being bent over double in the hot sun.

As the years passed, the stumps gradually rotted and could be pulled out of the ground. This left the fields clear enough to swing a long-handled scythe. But the farmer had to be careful — a careless swing and the blade of the scythe would break against a rock or, much worse, bounce back and gash a leg.

To help gather the cut wheat into sheaves for stooking, many farmers fitted their scythes with long wooden fingers. This device held, or cradled, the stalks of wheat until a large bundle could be dumped in one place, so it was called a cradle.

Chew Some Wheat Gum

Threshing was dusty work. To keep their mouths and throats moist and relatively clear of dust, farmers often chewed on a handful of grain. Chewing activated a substance in the grain called gluten, turning the mass into a gum-like wad. Children helping out in the field often stripped a handful of kernels out of the wheat to chew on. Another favourite chewing material was the gummy resin that oozed out of cut spruce wood.

Have a chew of pioneer gum. All you need is a handful of wheat kernels (available at health food stores). Put the wheat kernels in your mouth for a minute to moisten them, then chew. How does wheat gum compare with store-bought gum?

THE GRIST MILL

Wheat kernels are turned into flour by grinding them into meal, then sifting the meal to separate the fine white flour from the coarse, brown shorts (the hard shell of the kernel). Grain that is good enough to be ground into flour is called grist.

Because the kernels of grain are hard, grinding them takes a great deal of pressure. Over the centuries, people discovered that the most efficient way to produce large quantities of flour was to grind the kernels between two large, flat stones. The bigger and heavier the stones, the finer the flour and the greater the quantity that could be processed.

To turn these great millstones, millers harnessed wind power or water power. In a few areas, large windmills were set up. As the vanes (or arms) of the windmill rotated, they turned the millstones. However, most mills in North America were water-mills. To run them, water was diverted from a river into a millpond and held there by a dam. When the miller wanted to grind grain, he opened gates in the dam, which let the water flow past a water-wheel, turning it. The wheel turned a shaft that rotated the millstones.

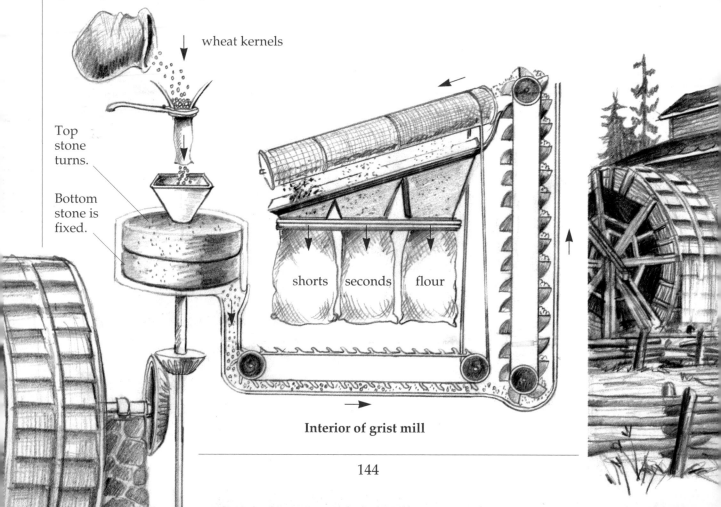

wheat kernels

Top stone turns.

Bottom stone is fixed.

shorts   seconds   flour

Interior of grist mill

144

As the millstones turned, the miller poured wheat kernels into a hole in the centre of the stones. The meal that poured out the bottom was sifted to separate the white flour from the shorts. In pioneer days, shorts were fed to the animals. Now people know that part of the shorts, the bran, adds fibre to their diets.

In the early days, backwoods families often lived far from the nearest mill. To obtain flour, the farmer might have to walk more than 30 km (20 miles) through the woods to the mill, carrying a 45-kg (100-pound) sack of grain. Then he faced the return journey with an equally heavy sack of flour on his shoulder.

The family's only alternative was to use a primitive handmill, which made small amounts of coarse flour. One kind was a sapling mill. The farmwife poured a shovelful of grain into a hollowed tree stump, then pounded it with a pounder. To ease this work, many early settlers rigged a bent sapling as a spring to help swing the mallet up. A slightly better handmill, called a quern, was made from two round, flat stones. One person turned the top stone with a wooden handle while a second person poured grain into a central hole. The flour was caught in a basket underneath. These methods produced a very coarse flour, but if the water-driven mill was too far away, they were the pioneers' only choices.

A VISIT TO THE GENERAL STORE

SARAH hummed to herself as the wagon jolted through the woods. She could hardly wait to get to the store. A letter was waiting for them! And Ma said she could sell her crock of butter. She'd have her very own money. Just like Meg.

"What are you going to buy?" Meg was sitting beside her, on the tail of the wagon, knitting needles clicking.

"Ribbons." Sarah had no doubts. For months she'd had her eye on the three spools set tantalizingly on the counter of Mr. Jamieson's store. But which colour — pink, yellow or white?

"You'll hardly get much of a length for that amount of butter." Meg sounded scornful. "Better do what I do and save up the credit."

"How much ribbon would I get?"

"Maybe enough to tie once around your braid with a bit of a bow. A waste of your money."

Just what Ma had said. "A nice stout piece of twine will do you fine," she'd added.

"Vanity, vanity," Granny clucked, so Sarah had stopped asking, but she hadn't stopped wanting. Pink? Yellow? Not white.

"Are *you* getting anything?" Sarah asked Meg.

"Dye for my wool. I want a nice deep red. Mrs. Jamieson said she'd have cochineal in by now."

How tiresome. Sarah changed the subject. "D'you suppose the letter's from Scotland?" They'd only ever had one letter from Granny's sister in Scotland.

"Mebbe." Meg sounded dubious.

The cousins in Nova Scotia, then? Sarah had been a baby when her parents moved the family here. She couldn't remember their farm at all, but she loved stitching together scraps of information from the letters and making up stories about the wonderful life she imagined her cousins living beside the sea.

"Are we nearly there?" she called.

"Nearly." Pa had said the same thing the last three times she'd asked. But this time it was true. As they came out of the trees, Sarah squinted at the sudden brightness. Ahead she could see a cluster of buildings along a slight widening in the track. Cleared fields stretched behind the village, but the forest pressed in on the other side of the road. First came the store, built of sawn wood just the way their new house would be, then an inn of squared logs and, at the end of the clearing, several rough log cabins that made up the tannery. The Jamieson family, with various aunts, uncles and cousins, ran all three.

Sarah jumped down as the wagon stopped in front of the store. Her legs felt all pins and needles from dangling over the tail of the wagon, and she had to hold on to the side rail and stamp her feet to make the feeling come back.

"Afternoon, Mrs. Brennan," Pa called to a woman climbing the steps to the store.

Maybe she has butter to sell, too, Sarah thought. What if Mr. Jamieson wants hers and not mine? She heard Granny's voice in her head, "Do unto others ..." and put the selfish thought out of her mind. But she *did* want to get into that store.

Grabbing her crock of butter, she darted up the steps. Her toe caught, she stumbled, and the crock flew out of her hands.

"Careful with your butter, dearie." Sarah looked up to see Mrs. Brennan holding out the crock to her. "Your ma won't be pleased if you spoil it on her."

"Oh, thank you for saving it," Sarah said as she followed Mrs. Brennan into the store. "I churned it myself and I'm to have the money from it. I wouldn't be able to buy my ribbons if I'd dropped it."

"Ribbon?" Mrs. Brennan sounded wistful. "You'll be having a good season with your cows, then. Mine didn't freshen so we've no milk at present."

"I'm sorry ..." What should she say next? Just then Meg and Pa came in, and Mrs. Brennan turned to talk to them.

Sarah skipped over to the counter and set her crock down. "Please, Mr. Jamieson, I'd like to sell my butter."

"Butter, is it? Made by your mother?"

"Made by myself. But my mother said it's as good as hers."

"Cow wasn't into the leeks now, was she?"

"Oh no, Mr. Jamieson. My mother would never have let me bring butter that tasted of leeks."

"There, there, young Sarah. Just teasing. Now — how much would you be wanting for it?"

"Well, I ..." Did *she* have to decide? Surely the storekeeper should set the price? "I'd want enough for some ribbon," she stated boldly.

"Ribbon, is it? Hard to come by. Costs a lot. Couldn't give you much. No more'n a handspan." He stretched his thumb and little finger apart.

Sarah gulped. Such a short piece? I don't care. I want it.

"What colour will you have?" As he spoke he turned away and reached under the counter. "Here you are, Mrs. Brennan. This'll be what you're after." He handed a letter over the counter. Sarah stared as Mrs. Brennan turned the sealed paper over and over, running her finger lovingly around the edges.

"Well then, young Sarah, what colour will you have?"

Sarah turned back to Mr. Jamieson. "I'm not sure. I'll have to think. Could I ... umm ... keep it on account, like Meg does, till I decide?"

"Sure could. I'll mark you down in my book." Mr. Jamieson scratched a line into the big ledger on the counter.

"Made up your mind yet?" Meg was tucking small parcels into her knitting bag.

Sarah sighed. "I guess you're right. Next time I'll ..." Out of the corner of her eye, Sarah caught sight of Mrs. Brennan handing the letter back to Mr. Jamieson. "What's she doing that for?"

"Sshh, she'll hear you," Meg whispered. "She can't afford to pay for it. Just comes in and looks at it every so often. From her mother back home, Mrs. Jamieson told me."

Sarah felt tears sting. "Oh, Meg, how dreadful."

Meg shrugged. "One of those things. Our letter's from the cousins, by the way. Pa says we have to leave it for Ma to open. You ready to go? Salt's all loaded on the wagon."

Sarah stared longingly at the shining tails unwinding from the spools of ribbon. Next time — next time I'll be able to get a really long piece. "I'm ready," she sighed and followed her sister out the door.

Pa had already turned the wagon. Sarah hitched herself up beside Meg on the tail.

"Haw, Buck, gee'long," Pa called, touching the near ox with his whip. The wagon started with a lurch. Sarah looked back at the store. Mrs. Brennan came out and stood for a moment on the porch, her shoulders drooping. Then she walked heavily down the steps.

Sarah felt her chest tighten, as though the breath had been squeezed out of her. The wagon jolted slowly towards the trees. Suddenly Sarah knew what she had to do. Jumping down, she said, "Just be a minute. I'll catch up with you."

She darted up the steps and into the store.

"Please, Mr. Jamieson, how much does it cost to fetch a letter?"

"Your pa's already fetched your letter. He's away out with it."

"It's Mrs. Brennan's letter I mean. Would my butter be enough?"

"Reckon so." Mr. Jamieson cocked his head at her quizzically.

Keeping her eyes steadfastly away from the ribbons on the counter, Sarah held out her hand. "I'll take it for her, then."

151

VISITING THE STORE

The Robertsons were lucky to have a village store only a two-hour wagon ride away. That meant all the essentials they couldn't grow or make on the farm were close at hand.

The storekeeper ordered goods from the city and had them delivered in barrels by wagon or boat. He made sure he had all the necessities: salt, spices, nails, tools such as axe heads and saws, gunpowder and lead balls for muskets and rifles.

He also stocked goods the settlers might want if they had a little extra money: cotton fabric, buttons, ribbons, thimbles, china dishes, special tools such as apple corers and, for school, slates to write on, slate pencils and spelling books. Sometimes the settlers asked the storekeeper to order special things. Sarah's father ordered glass panes for the windows in the new house. The glass, packed in straw in a barrel, took weeks to travel by boat and wagon from the city.

The 43.5 kg (96 pounds) of salt in this barrel would last one settler a year.

bolts of cotton fabric, often called calico, for caps, baby clothes and underclothes

Spices such as cinnamon sticks, cloves and nutmeg were packaged in paper twists.

scale

sticks of candy

slate pencils

keg of oysters from the Atlantic Provinces

The barrel on the left holds 119 L (31.5 gallons) of molasses. Containers were made in uniform sizes so they measured, as well as held, the contents.

axe heads packed in sawdust

the Robertsons' shopping list

1 Large barrel of salt
1 small packet of tea
1 paper of sewing needles
2 lbs. of gunpowder
Small pouch of tobacco
Small packet of dye
2 slate pencils

The storekeeper kept track of each person's account in a ledger. Because money was scarce, most people traded, or "bartered," things they had grown or made, such as wheat or ashes or butter, for store goods.

Customers brought their own containers — jugs, crocks, baskets, linen sacks.

Make a Balance Scale

The storekeeper weighed the amount each customer wanted on a scale. Here's how to make a simple scale.

You'll need:
- a metal skewer or nail
- 2 small yogurt containers
- 6 strings 25 cm (10 inches) long
- a coat hanger
- tape
- pennies for weights
- sugar

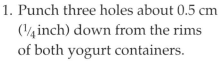

1. Punch three holes about 0.5 cm (¼ inch) down from the rims of both yogurt containers.

2. Thread one string through each hole and tie the ends.

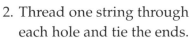

3. Tie one yogurt container onto each end of the hanger. Use tape to keep the string from sliding. Hang the hanger in a spot where the containers can hang free.

4. Make a set of weights out of pennies. Use a kitchen scale to measure 7 g (¼ ounce), 14 g (½ ounce) and 28 g (1 ounce) of pennies. Scoop some sugar into one container. Add pennies to the second container until the scale balances. How many pennies did you use? How much, then, does your sugar weigh? This is how early storekeepers weighed their goods.

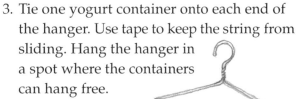

153

THE POST OFFICE

I t's your birthday. The letter carrier is coming up the walk. You reach out to take the envelope.

"That'll be forty cents, please," the letter carrier says.

What a shock! Paying to receive a letter!

That was how things worked in pioneer days. The Robertsons had to pay two shillings and eight pence (or about 48 cents) to get their letter. This was almost as much as a skilled labourer such as a cooper (barrel maker) would earn in one day.

Some settlers couldn't afford to claim longed-for letters. In 1838, in Brantford, Ontario, the postmaster had 48 unclaimed letters. To get around the high cost of postage, families in the backwoods often asked friends or neighbours travelling to towns and cities near their relatives to deliver their letters. Others used a code. Before leaving home, they arranged that Mother would send a blank page folded up as a letter. When the family heard a letter was waiting for them at the store, they knew all was well with Mother, and they could save themselves the cost of the postage. Others wrote coded messages on the outside of the letter. Whoever was visiting the store would just read the code and hand the letter back.

In 1851, Canada finally began issuing postage stamps. Under the new system, it cost only pennies for families to keep in touch.

First Canadian postage stamp, designed by Sandford Fleming and issued in 1851.

the new stove

the new bridge

154

near Dartmouth, N.S.

Dear Brother Robert, Mother and all there,
I write to let you know that we are all well
and hope these few lines will find you in as good
health as we are. The hay is almost in but there
has been so much stormy weather that we have got
along rather slow. Our planting looks first rate.
The corn has begun to spindle. Most of the beans
have podded. The potatoes are as large as eggs.
The house next over burned down. The men
put wet quilts on the barn and saved it.
We have built a bridge across the stream, so
you will know how that helps us to get our grain
to the mill. Well, our Jamie is off, gone for
a sailor on a merchant ship headed for
Barbadoes. They trade in molasses, sugar, coffee and
rum. We pray he will be safe. Our Sadie
will be married when the harvest is in. Her
intended has built them a nice snug cabin
on his father's land. Many says to tell you we
have one of the newfangled iron stoves and
it works a treat. Our little Janet wants you
to know she is doing well in school and can
spell down children twice her size. The boys are well.
Sad news from brother John's family. Their youngest was
taken with scarlet fever and couldn't be saved, although
the older children recovered. Well, I can't squeeze
many more words onto the page. Let us hear how
everything is with you when you have the time.
From your brother
Iain Robertson Esq.

155

WRITING THE LETTER

Can I write the letter back?" Sarah asked. "I can write small and neat now. I won't waste the paper."

Ma looked doubtful but Granny said, "Let her do the writing. I'll tell her what's to go down."

"We'll all tell her," Pa decided. "Each of us can have a sentence or two of news."

Sarah buys her paper at the store. She writes small and fills the whole of one side. Then she gives the paper a one-quarter turn and writes across the lines to squeeze in more news. This made it hard for the reader, but it *did* save on money for paper and postage.

New Bridgeford, Canada West, Sept. 10, 1840

Dear Uncle Iain, Aunt Mary and all,

I am writing for my family to thank you for your interesting letter. We are all well and glad to hear that you are the same. We were very sorry to hear the sad news about Uncle John's youngest. Granny says the baby is resting in the bosom of the Lord and we must be thankful for that. Our crops are in. Pa says to tell you we had a bumper year and hope you had the same. Next week we will have a working-bee to raise the walls of the new house. Ma and Meg are already making pies. Twenty are coming from around and about. Pa says we'll be moved in by Christmas. Willy and I helped by dragging stones for the cellar up the hill. The glass for the windows came all the way from Montreal. Only two panes were broke. Pa says to tell you there's new land being opened up north of us if your Andrew is looking to relocate.

Sarah makes her own ink (see her recipe on the next page).

She writes with a quill pen made from a turkey feather. Every so often she has to re-cut the end with a penknife. If she presses too hard while she's writing, the ink splatters.

To dry the ink, she sprinkles sand over the page, then blows it off.

When Sarah is finished, she will fold her paper to make its own envelope and seal it with a few drops of wax. If she's lucky, Pa will still have some proper sealing wax (mixed with red shellac to make it hard), but she will probably have to use plain candle wax.

Sarah's Homemade Ink Recipe

Mash walnut hulls and boil them until the water is a deep brown. Add vinegar and salt to the boiling water to set the colour. Add lampblack for a black colour. (To make lampblack, hold a small dish over a lit candle and collect the black soot.)

Signed and Sealed

To make a pioneer-style envelope, fold your letter like this:

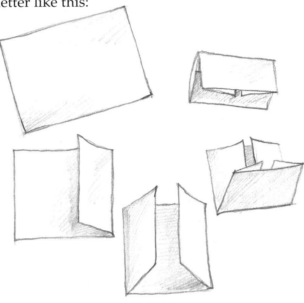

Seal it with a blob of wax from a candle. Ask an adult to light the candle for you.

Some people had seals to press their initials into the wax.

A broken seal meant someone else had read your letter. You can scratch your initials into the hardening wax with a pin, or twist a paper clip into a secret sign and use it as your own seal. For this you will need a thick blob of wax.

Let it cool until it is almost hard before you press your seal into it.

BUILDING THE
NEW HOUSE

Watch out!"

Willy jumped aside. A mallet whizzed past his ear and thudded to the ground right where he'd been standing. The man he'd been watching all morning swung down from the crossbeam of the frame he'd been anchoring to a post. "You'd best skedaddle outta here, son," he said to Willy as he scooped up the mallet. "Or you're gonna get hurt."

His second near disaster. And if Pa caught him idling about ... Willy retreated down the hill. Oh well, just watching's exciting. He hunkered down against the side of the barn, eyes searching for the man with the red neckerchief, the one who ran the crossbeams like a squirrel along a branch.

Neighbours who'd gathered to help with the house raising swarmed all over the building site. Mr. Simpson, an experienced house builder, was bossing the construction. From early morning he'd had men laying the floor timbers across the stone foundations. Now they were putting up the walls.

Pa had worked all summer preparing the frameworks for the walls. He'd also made pikes, long poles tipped with metal spikes, so the men could dig them into a frame and lift it. Willy had waited since early morning to see the walls go up. Now that one side was anchored, he didn't want to miss the rest.

"Willy! Where are you? You're supposed to help!" Sarah was emptying a pail of scrubbed potatoes into a huge kettle that hung from a tripod of logs. Over a second fire, four great roasts of pork sizzled on a spit. Turning the spit was supposed to be one of Willy's chores. But he wouldn't be able to see the action from there. And anyway, turning that spit was hot, heavy work. Willy edged farther into the shadow of the barn and ignored Sarah's complaints.

Up the hill, a dozen or so men surrounded a frame lying flat on the ground. "Heft — and up!" roared Mr. Simpson, and each one stooped, hooked a hand around the frame and hefted. Then they ran it over to the stone foundations, where more men were waiting with pikes.

"Right now — all together, boys." Mr. Simpson's powerful voice sang out. "Yo, heave — lift. Yo, heave — lift." On the command, the whole gang pushed together, and the heavy frame rose to the vertical. And there he was again — the man with the red neckerchief — shinnying up the post to guide home the crossbeams that joined the new frame to its neighbour.

"Willy! Willy Robertson! You get down here and help." This time it was Ma. Better not ignore *that*. Reluctantly, Willy turned his back on the engrossing scene.

A grim-faced Meg was turning the spit. "You get over here and do this," she said when Willy was close enough. "I need to help George." George had set up six kegs as table legs and now was struggling with a plank. Meg grabbed an end, and together they laid the plank across the kegs to make a trestle-table. As they started on a second table, Willy absent-mindedly leaned into the spit handle: Push, over the top, down and around. Push, over the top ... Even this far away the thunk, thunk, thunk reverberated right through him. If only he could be up there on a crossbeam, driving home trunnels with a mallet — right up there with the man wearing the red neckerchief. If only he could walk the crossbeams with no more care than you'd walk a log!

Sweat dripped into Willy's eyes, and he dropped the spit handle to swipe at them with his shirt-tail. The sizzle and spit of meat juices dripping into the fire gave off an aroma that made his stomach grumble. No point thinking about food. It would be a long time before the family got to eat.

The cabin door banged open, and Ma came out carrying two big jugs of maple syrup. The smell of pancakes frying drifted out with her. "Sarah will do that for a bit," she said, setting the jugs on one of the trestle-tables. "You help George and Meg bring all those stump stools out. Men'll want to eat shortly."

"Yes, Ma." Anything to get away from the spit.

Willy had just plunked the sixth stool down by the tables when a hand caught him by the back of the shirt and spun him around. The first thing Willy saw was the red neckerchief. The man from the crossbeam!

"Here, young fella, got a job needs doin'." The man mopped his brow and clapped his hat back on. "Need a man to cut and fetch us an evergreen tree. Just a little 'un. Say four — five feet tall."

A chance to help! Willy straightened up. "A tree? What for?"

The man gulped thirstily from a dipper of water, then wiped his mouth with the back of his hand. "Rafters'll be up soon. Gonna need a rooftree." He laughed at Willy's puzzled expression. "You never hearda that? It's for luck! Never you mind. I'll find someone ..."

"No!" Willy all but shouted. "I can do it."

"Good man. You have it back here in, say, quarter of an hour, and that'll be just dandy."

Pa's hatchet. I need Pa's hatchet, Willy thought, haring off in the direction of the woodpile.

"Willy!" Sarah called from the fire, where she was still turning the spit. "It's your turn."

"Can't. Got a building job to do." Ignoring her indignant wail, Willy snatched up the hatchet and ran. He knew just where to find the perfect tree — that pine at the edge of the beaver meadow.

Fifteen minutes later, Willy was dragging his prize across the farmyard. The men had been busy. The walls were up, and now two teams were racing each other to see which could nail on the most rafters. Just as Willy reached the foot of the hill, a great shout went up. The last rafter was in place.

"Here comes the lad." Hands grabbed Willy and hoisted him up on a strong shoulder. "Give it here." Willy boosted the tree up as high as he could. Hands took it and passed it up, then farther up, to the red-neckerchiefed man balancing on a crossbeam. "Good luck to this house!" he shouted as he lashed the tree in place, so that it stood up like a sentinel. Hats sailed through the air. Everyone cheered.

The jubilant winning team sat down to dinner first. As Willy hurried between the tables with pots of dandelion-root coffee and platters of sliced pork, hands ruffled his hair and clapped him on the shoulders.

"Well done, lad."

"That's a good tree you found us."

"There's a fine lad."

Willy thought he'd burst with happiness.

In the late afternoon the neighbourhood women arrived to help clean up and get ready for the evening party. By then the men had hammered the siding on the house and packed load after load of sawdust and aromatic wood shavings between the inner and outer walls, for insulation.

"It really looks like a house now," Sarah said when they finally had a minute to climb into their new kitchen.

"Roof still wants the shingling," Willy pointed out. He had helped Pa and George cut the shingles, and he wanted to see them in place. But his thoughts were all with the tree, standing straight as a flagpole on top. One day, he promised himself, it'll be me running the crossbeams, putting up the rooftree. Just like the man in the red neckerchief. Just like him.

PLANNING THE NEW HOUSE

The Robertsons had been planning the new house for over a year. Two years before, Mr. Robertson and his hired help had chopped down trees and used oxen to drag the logs to the sawmill. There the logs were sawn into planks and timbers.

sawmill

Back at the farm, the boys stacked the new lumber so that air could circulate between the layers. The lumber sat drying for a year. Well-seasoned lumber was important; otherwise, the wood might shrink, leaving gaping cracks in the walls.

Once the planting had been done in the spring, it was time to dig the cellar for the new house. George was old enough to help, but the Robertsons hired two men to make the back-breaking job go faster. As they dug the cellar hole, they also cut a ramp at one side. The oxen dragged the excavated earth up this ramp. Later, when the house was completed, the ramp would lead down to the root cellar.

A well-sweep helped remove the dirt from the well.

As soon as the cellar was finished, Mr. Robertson set his two hired men to digging a well. No more hauling water from the river.

Stones cleared from the fields had been dragged up the hill on stoneboats. These stones would become the cellar walls and the foundation for the whole house. Mr. Robertson asked a neighbour trained as a mason to build the cellar walls, to line the well with stones and to build a fireplace and chimney. This house had to last a lifetime, and Mr. Robertson wanted everything done just right.

While the mason sorted out the stones and cut them to size with his chisel and hammer, Willy and George helped their father make lime for mortar to cement the stones together. On a huge pile of dead branches in the middle of a newly cleared field, the boys piled chunks of limestone. George set the pile alight. Then the boys and Mr. Robertson tended the fire day and night until the last ember had burned out. A forest fire would be devastating to their little farm in the bush.

When the fire cooled, they raked the crumbling lumps of burnt limestone out of the ashes. These were mixed with water and sand to make mortar. Not all settlers had limestone on their land. Some settlers had to buy it from their neighbours.

While the mason worked on the cellar and the two hired men helped Mr. Robertson build the frames for the walls and roof, Willy and George finished the roof shingles. Last winter, Mr. Robertson had set aside four big cedar logs to dry. Cedar is waterproof and strong enough to make long-lasting shingles. Every spare day for the past year, Mr. Robertson and the boys had worked at the shingles. First, they cut the logs into 45-cm (18-inch) lengths, then split them into sheets using a froe and a mallet. George stacked these cedar shingles in a little shed to keep them dry.

mallet

froe

Mr. Robertson had a keg of wooden pins ready to fasten the shingles down. He had spent the winter evenings whittling them because he couldn't afford to buy all the iron nails such a big job would take. Iron nails were so valuable that people often burned down a house they were leaving and raked through the ashes to save the nails. To fasten the huge posts and beams that would hold the house up, Mr. Robertson fashioned dozens of pegs from seasoned oak. These trunnels, or treenails, were stronger than iron nails and wouldn't rust or bend. Buildings held together by trunnels have stood for over a hundred years.

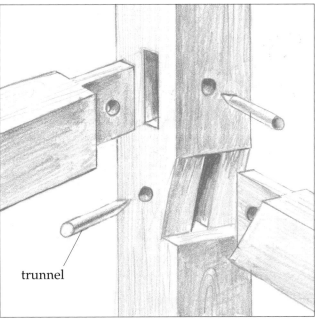

trunnel

At last everything was ready. As soon as the wheat was harvested, the Robertsons invited neighbours from miles around to help them raise the walls and put the roof on the new house.

Rollers, Levers, Runners and Ramps

Suppose you had to move a heavy box of books. Try lifting and carrying the box. Then try skidding it on a broom. Which is easier? Imagine if those books were huge stones. Hauling stones was familiar work on pioneer farms. People soon learned that dragging was easier than carrying.

In the early days in the bush, Mr. Robertson made a drag out of a small tree. Sometimes George and Willy did the dragging. For heavy loads, oxen did the work.

One winter, Mr. Robertson built a flat sled called a stoneboat. This was used to ferry stones as well as other heavy loads. A stoneboat was more useful than a wagon on a bush farm. Wagon wheels could get bogged down in the mud or broken off by half-rotted stumps, but the stoneboat could be dragged safely over bumpy ground.

Backwoods farmers had other ways of moving heavy loads. They turned logs and large branches into rollers, levers, runners and ramps. Try it yourself.

You'll need:
- a large book (a dictionary or encyclopedia volume)
- 4 pens or pencils (round, not straight-sided)
- 2 soup or dessert spoons
- a large can of soup (any flavour)
- a stack of 3 or 4 large books
- 2 rulers

1. Lift the large book to get a sense of how heavy it is. Put it on a table or other flat surface and, using one finger, push it forward.

2. Place the four pencils on the table, parallel to one another and about 5 cm (2 inches) apart. Carefully place the large book on top. Using one finger, push the book forward.

Which method is easier — with or without pencils? How can you keep the book rolling forward? Using *rollers*, people have moved houses from one site to another. The ancient Egyptians used rollers to move huge stones to build the pyramids.

168

3. Suppose you want to lift one end of the large book. Place a pencil parallel with the edge of the book and about 0.5 cm (¼ inch) away. Place the handle of the spoon under the edge of the book and lay the rest of the spoon over the pencil. Press down on the bowl of the spoon. What happens? The handle is acting as a *lever*, and the pencil is acting as a *fulcrum* (or pivot point) for the lever. Pioneers used a fulcrum and lever to pry out and lift heavy stones. Sweep wells used a fulcrum and lever to hoist full buckets of water out of wells.

4. Want another way to move the book? Slide two spoons, bowl-end first, well under one edge of the large book. Hold the spoon handles and skid the book around the table. Pioneers used similar *runners* to skid heavy loads over grass and snow-covered or icy surfaces.

5. Imagine you have just bought a barrel of molasses. To get it onto your wagon you have to lift it 1.5 m (5 feet). Impossible, you say? Turn a heavy plank into a *ramp*. Place the plank against the back of the wagon and roll the barrel up the ramp. Try it yourself. Lift a can of soup to feel how heavy it is. Set two rulers against the stack of large books to form a ramp. Use one finger to push the can up the ramp. Which took less force? Lifting the can or pushing it up the ramp?

Early settlers didn't have bulldozers, cranes and the other powerful equipment that builders have today. They had to rely on human strength (and a bit of science) to move huge logs, rocks and other heavy loads.

A NEW HOME IN THE BUSH

When Sarah and Willy were still babies, their parents decided to leave Nova Scotia and find land in the backwoods of Upper Canada. That winter, when the farm work was done, Mr. Robertson left his family behind and, taking his younger brother for company, set out to find a new home for them.

Mr. Robertson looked for land where walnut, chestnut and hickory trees grew — this was the best land for farming. Second best had maple, beech and cherry. Too many cedar and hemlock trees meant swampy ground.

When Mr. Robertson found land with a mix of good trees and a river running through it, he searched for the surveyor's stake that marked one corner of the property. This told him the lot and concession number. Then he followed the marks the surveyor had blazed on trees until he had walked all around the boundaries of the 40-ha (100-acre) lot. Satisfied that this would make a good farm, he went to the land agent's office in town, where he identified the land by its lot and concession number on the surveyor's map. The deeds of ownership were drawn up, and Mr. Robertson paid for the land.

The next job was to cut down trees and build a shelter so Mr. Robertson could bring his family out. First the brothers built a shanty to live in while they cleared some land. This was a rough hut with hollowed basswood logs fitted together to make a waterproof roof. (Later, when a log cabin had been built, the cow and pig lived in this shanty until a barn was built. Then it was used as a chicken coop and a storehouse.)

the first shanty

LAND AGENT

170

With the help of some neighbours, the brothers built a log cabin. When the house-building bee was over, the brothers had a rectangular house of logs 7.3 m by 3.7 m (24 feet by 12 feet). They had to chop holes for a door and windows. At first the windows were covered with animal hides greased to let in a little light. The door was made of rough planks, and the hinges were pieces of leather. Later, Mr. Robertson made a better-fitting door and bought glass for the windows. Mr. Robertson was determined to have a wood floor before his family arrived. He had stayed in cabins with dirt floors and knew how cold they were in the winter and how muddy they could become in the spring.

Next the Robertsons needed a barn. The plan was simple: two square log buildings with a space between. The roof covered both the buildings and the space in between. This roofed-in space would be the threshing floor. Over the years, more sections were added to stable cows, oxen and, eventually, a horse. On the leeward side of the barn (away from the wind), the Robertsons built a corral for the sheep. To make the corral warm as well as safe from wolves, they wove a fence out of willow branches.

The Robertsons lived in the cabin for nearly eight years. As the children grew, the family felt more and more crowded. One day Mr. Robertson came home from the village with wonderful news. Up the river, a sawmill was opening. With an easy way to turn their logs into boards, they could build the new, big house they'd been dreaming about. The old cabin would become a workshop for Mr. Robertson and the boys.

building the log cabin

the barn

THE CORNHUSKING BEE

Bee, a bee, a bumblebee
Stung a man upon his knee
And a hog upon the snout!
O-u-t says you are OUT!

The pointing finger stopped at Sarah. Squealing with excitement, she skipped into the middle of the circle, dodging the blindfolded Rachel. The girls zigged and zagged while the circle of children danced around them yelling "Hot! Cold! Hot! Cold!" Sarah felt dizzy. She twisted out from under Rachel's grasping fingers and fled, but the circle of boys and girls closed around them. There was nowhere to run.

A hand grabbed her arm. "Got you! Got you, Sarah Robertson," Rachel shrieked as they both toppled onto another girl. In a laughing tangle of bodies, the circle broke up.

When have I ever had such fun, Sarah wondered, lying panting on the floor. The barn looked odd from that angle. Around the threshing floor, light flickered from tin lanterns hung on the tines of up-ended pitchforks. Close by, Mr. Burkholder and three of his cronies sat on stump stools, chewing on straws. Gossiping, she decided. In the far corner, another game of blind man's buff was starting. Near her, Willy was hitting conkers with a boy she didn't know.

In the centre of the floor, the serious work was under way. Meg and George and the other young people of the community were husking the Burkholders' corn. They worked in teams, furiously tearing off husks and throwing the cobs on a quickly mounting pile. As the hill of unhusked corn shrank, the two teams worked faster and faster, each determined to finish with the bigger pile of husked cobs.

Suddenly a boy jumped up waving a red ear of corn. "I got one, I got one! Meg Robertson, I pick you!"

"Oh no you don't, Josh Turner." Meg scrambled up and ran. Josh leaped over the pile of husks brandishing the red ear like a trophy. "I gets a kiss," he shouted, dashing after her. "I gets a kiss."

"Watch out, Meg," Sarah shrieked, seeing Josh close the gap.

Meg stopped and turned. Just as Josh reached out, she gave a mighty shove. Josh teetered backwards, landing in a mound of husked corn. Ears flew everywhere.

"You've wrecked it, you dummy. Wrecked it!" voices howled.

Meg stood triumphant, hands on hips, watching Josh crawl away from the scattered corn. "Next time, Josh Turner," she called after him, "you ask first!"

GETTING READY FOR WINTER

October and November were busy months on a backwoods farm. Food to last the winter had to be stored in the root cellar and storage room. Candles to light the dark days had to be made, and animals that couldn't be fed through the winter had to be slaughtered and the meat salted away or smoked to feed the family.

Some jobs were too big for just one family, so a neighbourhood bee was held to get the work done. Everyone looked forward to apple paring, cornhusking, quilting and taffy-pulling bees, sometimes called frolics. After the work was done, the young people danced or played courting games such as musical chairs, in which the last two to grab a chair had to kiss. If a fiddler lived nearby, he'd be asked to play, but often the music came from rhythmic chanting or harmonicas made from paper folded over a comb.

salting meat

food for the root cellar

making candles

after the work

176

A Homemade Fiddle

Early settlers thought up many ways of providing the rhythm and beat necessary for a barn dance. They made banjos from dried gourds, rhythm instruments from blocks of wood and simple fiddles from a string and a stick. Try playing this version of a homemade fiddle.

You'll need:
- a hammer
- a nail
- an empty 1.36-L (48-ounce) can with one end removed
- scissors
- heavy string
- a pencil

1. Ask an adult to help you use the hammer and nail to punch a hole in the middle of the bottom of the can. Remove the nail.

2. Cut a length of string that reaches from your waist to the floor.

3. Tie a large knot at one end. Thread the string through the hole in the can so that the knot catches on the inside.

4. Tie the other end of the string around the middle of the pencil.

5. To play your "sound bow," place the can on the floor. Put one foot on top to hold it in place. Curl your fingers around the pencil and pull the string tight. Pluck the string with the forefinger of your other hand. Change the pitch by loosening and tightening the string.

STORING FRUITS AND VEGETABLES

In the days before refrigerators and canned food, people needed ways to "put by" (store) today's plenty against tomorrow's shortage.

Potatoes, turnips and other root vegetables were stored raw, in a root cellar or in a pit in the ground. Each fall, Mr. Robertson lined a pit 1.5 m (5 feet) deep with straw, then half filled it with potatoes. He packed more straw on top and buried everything under 60 cm (2 feet) of earth to keep the potatoes cold but not so cold that they would freeze. He stuck a hollowed basswood tube into the pit to get rid of gas that might otherwise build up and rot the potatoes.

In the new house, the Robertsons would have a real root cellar, a stone-walled room under the kitchen. In many houses the entrance was from an outside door and staircase. Some houses had a trapdoor and ladder from the kitchen. The root cellar kept root vegetables just above freezing in the winter. In summer the cellar was cool enough to keep milk and butter from spoiling.

Halfway through the winter, when the family had used all the potatoes in the house, the pit was opened. If the pit was deep enough and warm enough, the potatoes would be firm. Inexperienced pioneers smelled rotting potatoes as they lifted off the straw covering and knew they had a hungry few months ahead.

Fruits, such as apples, needed to be handled with care if they were to last. When the apples were ripe, the family picked the best ones carefully, twisting, not pulling, each apple from the twig. They packed each apple into its own straw nest in a barrel to keep, unbruised, for winter eating. Then the rest of the apples were stripped from the tree. Some were taken to a cider mill, where the juice was pressed out of them and made into cider and vinegar. Others were cooked down to make applesauce and apple butter. But most were cut into slices, threaded onto strings or sticks and hung near the fire to dry. During the winter, the dried apples would be soaked in maple syrup, then baked into pies. No wonder apple trees were never cut for firewood; they were too valuable.

Drying Apples

Dried apple slices make good snacks. Try some yourself.

You'll need:
- a peeler
- 2 or 3 apples
- a paring knife
- cookie sheets

1. Peel the apples. Ask an adult to cut them into quarters, remove the core and slice the quarters into thin slices.
2. Spread the slices on the cookie sheets so that the slices do not overlap.
3. Turn the oven to 70°C (150°F). Wearing oven mitts, place the trays of apple slices in the oven.
4. Your apple slices will take six hours or longer to dry. Once every hour, take the cookie sheets out of the oven and turn the slices so they will dry evenly, then put them back in the oven. Always use oven mitts when handling the cookie sheets.
5. At the end of six hours, take two slices out of the oven and let them cool. Test the slices by squeezing them. If they leave moisture on your fingers, they are not yet dry. Leave the cookie sheets in for another hour and test again.
6. Store the dried fruit in tightly covered containers or plastic bags. Eat the slices as snacks or add them to your morning cereal.

MEAT FOR THE WINTER

Through the summer the hogs rooted for their food in the woods or anywhere they could find a tasty morsel. By late fall they were big enough to slaughter. Hogs supplied lard for cooking and most of the meat the family ate for the following year.

On butchering day, the Robertsons were up well before dawn. Everyone had a job to do. Willy and George lugged pails of water to fill the cauldron, which was set over a fire. Meg and Sarah got out big bowls, knives and cutting boards. Granny took Lizzie and Tommy into a bedroom to keep them out of the way. Mr. Robertson sharpened knives while he waited for Mr. Burkholder to arrive.

Slaughtering was too big a job for one man. Another day, he would help the Burkholders with their slaughtering.

In the cabin, Sarah was filling a large kettle with water when she heard the loud squeals. Then it was quiet. She poured more water into the kettle. Soon they would be very busy.

Out in the yard, Willy watched his father and Mr. Burkholder lower the carcass into the cauldron. The boiling water loosened the hair and bristles. Willy didn't mind scraping the bristles from the hide. He and George were allowed to trade them at the general store. The storekeeper sold the bristles to brushmakers or to travelling shoemakers, who used them as flexible needles.

Mr. Robertson set the two hams in tubs of brine and molasses to marinate (soak up the flavours) for several weeks. Then he hung them inside the chimney, well up from the flames, where the smoke would cure (preserve) them. When he had time, he planned to build a special smokehouse like Mr. Burkholder's, where he could cure many hams at once.

While the men cleaned the carcass, Mrs. Robertson and Meg were busy over the fire in the cabin. In one kettle they carefully boiled down the lard, skimming off the scum, then ladling the liquid fat into stone jars to cool and harden. Meanwhile, the hog's head and feet simmered in another kettle. Later, the liquid and tender meat would be turned into a delicious jellied loaf called scrapple. The recipe, a German specialty, came from Mrs. Burkholder.

When the men finished cleaning the carcass, they set aside two big hams for smoking. The rest of the meat was cut into meal-sized chunks and stored in a large barrel. Over each layer of meat a generous portion of salt was sprinkled. Then the barrel was topped up with strong brine (salt dissolved in water) and sealed.

Mrs. Robertson and Meg chopped the leftover scraps of meat, seasoned them with salt and herbs, then stuffed them into sausage casings made from the cleaned and washed intestines.

That evening for supper the Robertsons had fried liver — one of the few times in the year they enjoyed fresh meat.

JERKY AND PEMMICAN

The Native people taught the early settlers other ways to preserve meat. They cut venison into thin strips, smoked it and let it dry in the sun. The dried strips, called jerky, could be stored in birch-bark containers for months without spoiling. Because jerky was lightweight and nutritious, it was perfect for travellers. Explorers, *coureurs de bois*, *voyageurs* and trappers were nourished by the chewy jerky as they crossed and recrossed the country.

The Native people often powdered the jerky, added nuts, seeds or dried berries and mixed it all with melted fat. Rolled into balls and stored in a cool dry place, this pemmican also kept for months. It had the added advantage of containing vitamin C from the berries. A handful added to a pot of boiled cornmeal made a tasty porridge.

SALT

Why did Mr. Robertson use so much salt when he was storing the meat? The bacteria that cause meat to spoil cannot live in brine. In the days before refrigeration, salt was the only safe preservative for meat.

Salt was used for other things, too. Eggs buried in salt would stay fresh enough for baking although not for boiling or frying. Because salt is a good cleanser, wooden floors and tabletops were often scoured with it. When teeth needed brushing, Mrs. Robertson would fray the end of a small twig, dip it in salt and scrub her children's teeth — as often as once a week! Salt was even used to clean animal hides being tanned to make leather.

Where did all this salt come from? The Robertsons bought barrels of salt from the general store. These barrels had been shipped by canal and wagon from saltworks — factories built beside salt springs — where the brine was boiled until the water evaporated, leaving behind salt crystals. People who lived close to the ocean made salt by evaporating sea water in large, flat pans. It took 1136 L (300 gallons) of sea water to make 32 kg (70 pounds) of solar salt, as this kind of salt is called. In other places, deposits of rock-salt were mined from the earth.

Every community, large or small, needed tonnes (tons) of salt each year. Lack of salt often slowed down the settlement of an area. People wouldn't buy land unless there was a general store fairly close by to supply them with salt.

In pioneer times, salt bought by the barrel at the general store was damp and lumpy. A bowlful of salt chunks was placed near the fire to dry out. Then one of the children would crush the lumps with a rolling pin. This fine salt was stored in a small salt box on the mantelpiece for everyday use.

EVERYTHING BUT THE SQUEAL

Every part of the hog was turned to good use on a pioneer farm. Lard (the soft fat from the pigs) was especially useful for lighting and soap making.

For special occasions, Mrs. Robertson made dipped or moulded candles from tallow (beef or sheep fat) and beeswax. (To see how candles were dipped, turn to page 226.) She stored all her candles in a tin box to keep them safe from mice. Candles were too precious to waste.

a tin candle box

A spoonful of lard served as fuel for a metal-dish lamp called a cruisie, but these little lamps didn't throw much light.

For a better light, the pith was stripped from inside cattail stems and dipped in lard. These rushlights were smoky and smelly, but they were fine for everyday use.

Lard was also used to make soap. The other ingredient in soap was lye. To make the lye, Mrs. Robertson saved ashes from the fire. Rainwater poured over the ashes dissolved and carried away lye (alkali) from the ashes.

The lye-water was emptied into a huge pot along with lard, fat scraps, drippings and candle ends. The mixture had to be stirred as it boiled. It was hot work and hard on the eyes because the lye gave off irritating fumes.

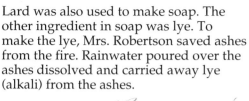

When the liquid thickened and turned jelly-like, Mrs. Robertson ladled it into stone crocks. She kept a jug of this slimy soap by the wash-basin for everyone to use as they came in from working in the fields.

On wash day she added several cupfuls to the laundry, which was boiled in the same cauldron she used to make the soap.

A barrel of ashes and 5.5 kg (12 pounds) of fat made 18 kg (40 pounds) of soap — enough to last a family for a year. Mrs. Robertson often took a jug of soft soap as a gift to welcome a new family to the neighbourhood. She knew from experience they wouldn't have the ingredients to make this most necessary item until they had hogs to slaughter.

SHADOW STORIES

Wind whistled through the cracks around the door, but Sarah felt warm and cosy on the settle. She was amusing Lizzie with a game of jacks. The rest of the family was gathered around the fire doing little chores until bedtime. George whittled pieces of kindling into shavings to start tomorrow morning's fire. Ma and Meg stitched pieces for a new quilt. Willy was busy with a special project, shaving a hickory branch to make a broom for the new house. "Tell us a story, Gran," he asked, drawing his knife down the branch carefully, so the splint wouldn't break off.

Gran put her knitting down and stretched her fingers. The flickering firelight caught them and sent long thin shadows dancing over the wall. "Ah, those shadows remind me of a good one." Everyone perked up expectantly. Even Pa laid down the boot he'd been waterproofing with lard.

"Have I told you the one about the hobgoblin that lived up the glen from us?"

"Tell it again," said George. He brushed the shavings into a basket and settled himself more comfortably on his stool.

Sarah scooped the jacks into her apron pocket and pulled Lizzie closer. They snuggled together as Granny started.

"My granny used to tell how this one and that one up the glen would have a wee elf to help with the work. For no more than a sup of milk or a crust of bread left on the hearth each night, the hobgoblin would tidy and fetch, make the butter come quickly and the bread rise evenly. Lucky the wife who had such a helper. But some folk don't know when they're well off. Farmer Donald's wife, who lived no more than a stone's throw up the glen from us, was such a one. That wee elf made life very easy for her, but was she happy? Always complaining, she was. No sooner would the hobgoblin fetch in the water than she'd say, 'Oh, if only he'd fetched in the kindling.' No sooner had a bundle of sticks appeared than she'd say, 'Oh, if only he'd sweep the hearth.' And so it went, day after day.

Soon the woman did nothing but sit in her chair crying 'If only ...' and the hobgoblin was flying about doing everything. Then one day, the cry changed. 'If only he didn't eat so much,' she said, and that night she put out only half a crust of bread. 'If only,' she said the next day, 'if only he didn't drink so much,' and put out only half a saucer of milk. And so it went, with the poor hobgoblin getting less and less each day and still doing all the work."

Sarah felt Lizzie's head pressing harder and harder into her shoulder. She looked down. Lizzie had her thumb in her mouth and was sucking furiously. Her eyes, wide as saucers, stared straight at Granny. Sarah cuddled her closer. She remembered that feeling, half scared, half fascinated, when Granny got to telling about the odd things that happened back in Scotland.

Granny looked around the circle and her voice dropped. "Then came a night when Donald's wife left *nothing* on the hearth for the goblin to eat. The next day, no matter how often she cried 'If only ...' no work was done. Still she hadn't learnt her lesson, for that evening she went to bed again without leaving a morsel or a sup for the wee elf. In the middle of the night she woke to a terrible clatter. She ran to the front room to see pots and pans flung about the room and ashes from the fire scattered all over the hearth.

"'I washed for you and fetched for you,' a little voice screeched, 'and nothing would you give me. So there's for *you*.' And a pot sailed across the room and smashed the one glass window in the little house. As the moonlight streamed in, Donald's wife saw the shadow of the wee elf capering and dancing about the room, then out the door it went. That was the last she saw of him, and from then on not a thing went right in her kitchen — the milk soured, the bread baked hard as stone, the well went dry and her kindling was always too green to light."

Granny looked around again, sizing up her audience's reaction.

"So if ever," she started in a warning voice, "if ever you see a hobgoblin, you be sure to treat it right. Look, Lizzie, there's one now." Granny held her hand in front of the fire, twisting and turning it, and suddenly, across the wall danced an imp of a creature.

With a cry Lizzie hid her face against Sarah's arm.

"You're scaring the child," Pa said. "Look, Lizzie. Look what I can do." He made a fist in the firelight, and there on the wall was a rabbit's head. "Look, Lizzie," he coaxed, and the silhouette changed to a barking dog, then a goose.

"Do it again," Lizzie crowed, her fears forgotten. "Do it again."

HOMEMADE FUN

The early settlers had to make their own fun. On winter evenings, the younger children played games like jacks or crokinole or checkers. The pieces were made from anything they had on hand — dried corncobs, nuts, bones or carved scraps of wood.

The adults often combined work and play. Boys and men whittled shavings to start the fire next day, then turned another piece of wood into a toy for the baby. Girls and women knitted stockings and mittens or pieced tiny scraps of material together to make squares for bed quilts.

Sitting around the fire at night, their one free time, they listened to grandparents spin stories about life in the old country or tell about the funny, sad or scary things that had happened to people they'd known or heard about. Ghost stories or tales of supernatural happenings were extra scary when told by the flickering light of the fire.

Shadow Shapes

Firelight was good for making shadow shapes on the wall. You can do the same thing with a flashlight. In a darkened room, ask a friend to point a flashlight at a blank wall. Hold your hands about 1 m (3 feet) in front of the flashlight. Move your hands towards or away from the wall until you get the clearest shadows. Using the hand-y diagrams below, throw shadows of various animals. Move your fingers to make the dog bark or the rabbit twitch its nose.

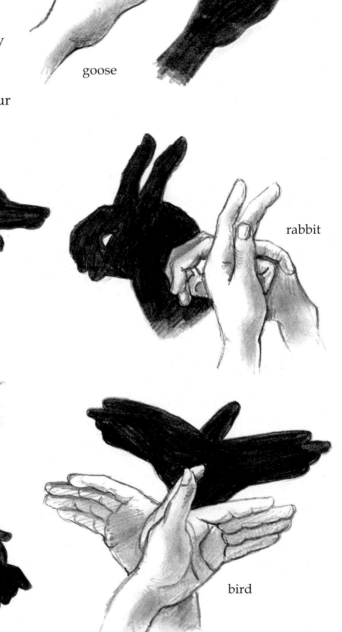

goose

dog

dog

rabbit

man

bird

Shadow Puppets

The moving pictures of pioneer times were shadow puppets. With a candle, a sheet tacked over a wooden frame and cutout figures, children brought folk tales and legends to life. The Robertson children acted out the Scottish tales their granny told. You can use the story about the hobgoblin or choose one you already know.

You'll need:
- tacks or a stapler
- a piece of white sheet
- a wooden frame at least 36 cm x 46 cm (14 inches x 18 inches) — a large picture frame works
- a hammer and nails
- a piece of wood at least 10 cm (4 inches) wide to use as a base for the frame
- Bristol board or other cardboard
- scissors
- tape
- Popsicle sticks or short pieces of stiff wire
- brass paper fasteners
- a gooseneck lamp

1. Ask an adult to help you make a screen by tacking or stapling the sheet tightly across the frame. Then nail on the base so the screen will stand on a table.

2. To make the puppets, draw your characters on the cardboard. Draw them in profile (standing sideways), to show their facial features. Cut them out.

3. Tape a Popsicle stick or rod made from wire to the back of your cutouts.

4. If you want an arm or a leg to move, cut that piece separately and join it to the body with a brass fastener. Attach a separate Popsicle stick or rod to each moving part.

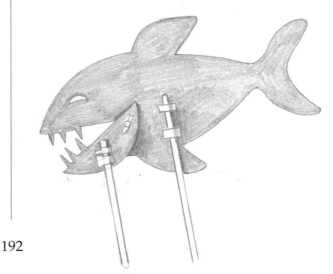

5. Put the screen on the table so that the outer edge of the screen is flush with the table edge, as shown. Set the lamp about 1 m (3 feet) behind the table.

6. Hold your puppet flat against the screen. To give the effect of walking, move the puppet up and down slightly at the same time as you move it across the screen. Keep it flat against the screen at all times, so the audience will see a dark silhouette. Experiment with the puppets. Make a bird fly, a fish swim, an angry character jump up and down.

7. Once you feel comfortable using the puppets, rehearse your play. Organize your scenes so that no more than two or three puppet operators are behind the screen at one time.

At school you can use an overhead projector for your light source. This also allows you to project scenery onto the screen. Draw the scenery onto sheets of acetate with acetate markers.

FEEDING THE FIRE

Boys in a pioneer household had many chores, but their most important one was keeping their mother supplied with wood for the fire.

First the men of the household hauled logs from the woods and used a two-man saw to cut them into lengths to fit the fireplace. These log sections were stacked to dry; wet wood is very difficult to chop.

When they were dry, some of the logs were split to make cordwood. To do this, the chopper wedged a log upright into a chopping block made from the forked crotch of a large tree. Experienced choppers knew enough to chop down the sides of each log, splitting small sections off. If they tried to split the log with a mighty swing into its centre, the blade of the axe might stick fast in the wood.

Every day the boys of the household carried in cordwood to fill the wood box that stood beside the fireplace. Every evening, as the family sat around the fire before going to bed, one of the boys would shave a stick of cordwood into kindling to coax the fire into life the next morning.

To make sure the fire stayed alive all night, the boys rolled an oak log into the cabin each evening and shoved it to the back of the fireplace. Oak burns slowly and gives off few sparks, so it is the safest wood to have as a backlog. The remains of the day's fire were covered with ashes to keep the embers smouldering. In the morning, the embers were coaxed into a flame by blowing on them, then feeding them shavings.

If the fire went out, there were only two ways of restarting it. One was to use flint and iron to strike a spark. With luck this spark would set tinder (usually charred linen or dry moss) on fire. The easier way was to send a child to the nearest neighbour to bring live coals back in a small iron pot. Many a pioneer child trudged all the way to the neighbours' and back, blowing on the coals to keep them glowing, scared that any minute they would snuff out.

iron

flint

tinder

In winter, when the family needed more than embers to keep the cabin warm, one of the boys sat up all night tending the fire.

Chopping wood was a never-ending chore. Because the fire had to be kept going day and night, wood chopped into lengths was stacked all around the cabin. To keep it neat and to help it dry, the wood was stacked in cords 1.2 m (4 feet) deep, 2.4 m (8 feet) long and 1.2 m (4 feet) high. The Robertsons needed 50 to 70 cords of wood a year to do all the cooking and to keep their one big room reasonably warm in winter.

THE WOODSMAN'S AXE

T ake good care of this," Pa said when he handed Willy the axe. "Keep it sharp and don't let it rust."

Willy was thrilled to be given his very own axe. He promised himself he would always remember what his father had told him: Don't leave your axe out where someone can step on it; when you're finished with it, wedge it into a block of wood; rub it with fat at the end of each day to keep it from rusting; if it's cold out, heat the axe before you use it.

In the early years on a backwoods farm, the axe was often the settler's only tool. With it he felled logs for his cabin, cleaned out brush to plant a garden, split cordwood for his fire, shaved dry sticks for kindling and even, by holding the freshly sharpened axe blade in his palm, whittled little figures. He could do jobs big and small as long as he kept his axe blade keen-edged and free of rust. Although a well-looked-after blade would last for decades, the handle often broke, so every good axeman kept a billet of ash or hickory seasoning near the fire, waiting to be shaped into a new handle.

LOST IN THE WOODS

What am I going to do? Willy asked himself as he trudged through the woods behind George. Fear squeezed his chest and his breath came in short, shallow pants. We should have stayed at the Simpsons'. I knew it was too late to start back.

George tramped on into the fading light, slashing at bushes with his stick, spraying snow behind him. If only I could see better, Willy thought. He rubbed at his eyes, his mittens rough with ice pellets where he'd wiped his nose. If I could prove to him … And then he saw it. Just what he'd been afraid of.

"Wait, George," he called. "Stop." He ran ahead and reached for his brother's arm. George shook him off impatiently. "Stop, I said." Willy could hardly believe he'd spoken to George that way, but it worked. George stopped and turned, scowling.

"Look," Willy pointed at the tracks. "I can tell by that mark across the heel. It's the same as the one on your boot. Nekeek told me what to look for." Willy swallowed hard to keep himself from bursting into tears. "We're following our own trail. We're lost."

"Stop whining. I know right where we are," George shouted.

"No you don't. I'm not going one step more."

"Oh yes you are, crybaby." George grabbed the back of Willy's coat and shoved him ahead. "I'm not telling Pa I left you behind in the woods."

I'm right, Willy told himself, wrapping his left arm around a sturdy sapling. He dug in his heels as George dragged at his right arm. "I told you we should've started sooner."

"If you say 'I told you' one more time ..." George's face, red with anger, made Willy swallow his next words. I won't take one more step, he thought. Going round in circles just wears out your strength — that's what Nekeek's uncle says, and he should know.

Willy saw George's teeth clench and braced himself, but suddenly George turned away. Something defeated-looking about the slump of George's shoulders made Willy say, "Someone'll come to find us."

"Yeah? Who? Who knows we're here?"

Willy's heart sank. George was right. Their parents wouldn't worry for hours yet, and the Simpsons wouldn't even know something was wrong. We should've started back earlier, Willy wailed to himself. He wanted to say it out loud, to hurl it at George. Your fault, your fault, your fault.

"We can't stay here," George muttered. "We'll freeze. We've got to keep moving. Come on." He started to trudge along the trail again.

"Wait," Willy called, letting go of the tree trunk. "I know what to do."

"You?" The scorn in George's voice was the last straw.

"You always think you know everything, George. Well, this time you don't. Nekeek's uncle — "

"Nekeek's uncle!" George howled. "Don't you start that again." George lunged at Willy and began to shake him. "I'm sick to death of hearing about Nekeek's uncle."

"Let go." Willy wrenched himself away and stood panting, fists clenched. Suddenly all the steam seemed to go out of his brother. "Come on," George muttered, turning again towards the darkening woods. "Keep moving. Keep warm."

Willy stood where he was as George tramped away, not looking back. Soon he had disappeared into the darkness. Willy felt a panicky impulse to call out "Wait for me!" No, he told himself. I know what to do. Nekeek showed me. He took a deep breath to calm himself, then dug into the pocket where he kept his jackknife. Too bad it's not bigger. He thought ruefully about the two hunting knives they'd taken to sharpen on the Simpsons' whetstone. George had both strapped to his belt. Nothing he could do about that. Work fast, he told himself. Six stout sticks, lots of evergreen branches, and he could make a nice snug shelter. He looked around. Near the trail stood several small spruce. Branches first, Willy thought, striding towards them.

Hacking with a jackknife and tearing with his hands left him hot and panting, despite the cold night air. But the sweat turned clammy on his forehead when he stopped to catch his breath. By the time he had a pile of spruce boughs, his hands were scratched and bleeding. He gathered the boughs up in his arms and staggered back to the trail.

Where should he build the shelter? He threw down the branches and looked around. Nekeek's uncle said always keep your back to the wind, build into the side of a hill. Not so easy here, Willy thought. But those two saplings are close together. Maybe I could use them for the uprights.

Some fallen branches lay on the forest floor. He chose a stout one and tried it between the saplings. Too long to wedge between them. He marked where to cut and began sawing at the bark with his jackknife. The blade was dull now. On his knees, he pressed the branch against a rock and sawed away. The knife blade made a thin, squealing sound against the moist inner wood, but no matter how hard he pressed, the blade cut no deeper. He stopped and took a deep breath, swallowing the panic that kept rising in his throat. If he didn't get this shelter built, he might freeze to death, just as George said. What should he do? Perhaps he could break the branch along the cut line. Perhaps if he braced it against the rock and stomped on it …

As he straightened, he heard a sound. He stood rigid, listening into the dark night. The woodland was eerily silent, but he was sure he'd heard something. What animals prowled on a winter's night? There it was again, a rustling sound like something scuffling through snow-covered leaves. His heart lurched painfully. How could he protect himself from a wolf or a wildcat? His hand gripped the little knife.

He peered at the darkness and suddenly saw George, half hidden by a tree, staring at him.

Willy let out a shaky breath. "I was trying to cut this branch — for a crosspiece," he said, as though George had been working with him all the time.

"Nothing to that." George's voice was too loud in the silent forest. "Give it here." He reached for the branch. Willy almost refused. This is my shelter, he wanted to say. But the look on George's face was not the old bullying look. Working together, they soon had the crosspiece wedged between the saplings. They rested more branches against the crosspiece, then covered them with boughs, forming a tent.

"Nice and snug," Willy said, crawling over the spruce boughs they had spread inside. "We could pile snow on top and be even warmer."

"What we need is a fire." George had crawled in beside him. They sat cross-legged, peering at each other in the dark. "Maybe we could use my knife to strike some sparks off that rock." But he didn't sound enthusiastic.

Willy yawned. "Hard work, building a shelter." His stomach rumbled. Try not to think about food. They'd had a big meal at the Simpsons', but that must have been hours ago. A hot drink would be nice.

"Remember that time Uncle Iain got lost in the woods and climbed a tree so's a wildcat wouldn't jump him? Imagine trying to hang onto a branch all night."

"And that time Meg left the cow in the woods all night 'cause she was too scared to go after it in the dark?"

"Yeah, and remember — " A great yawn cut off Willy's next words. His head nodded. He could hardly keep his eyes open.

The next thing he knew, a grey light was seeping into the shelter. He and George were huddled in a warm knot on the spruce boughs.

Willy untangled himself and crawled out of the shelter. His legs felt stiff and numb. He stretched, then jigged up and down to limber up. The light was brightening quickly. Soon they'd be able to scout around the woods for the trail they'd missed the night before.

"D'you hear something?" George was standing beside him. Willy listened. From far off came the blare of a horn.

"Pa's hunting horn!" They set up a shout that echoed through the woods. "We're here! We're here!"

The sound of the horn got louder and louder. Suddenly there was Pa, coming through the trees.

"Well, you two, what a fright you've given us. Just a minute till I give the signal so the others'll know you're found." He gave three short blasts on the horn, followed by two long ones. From far away came the answering blast of another horn.

"What's this, then?" Pa was walking around the shelter, studying it from all angles. "Well now, that's a clever wee house. How did you boys know to make that?"

Willy looked at George. Did he dare mention Nekeek's uncle?

"Willy did it." George's tone was nonchalant. "Something he learned from Nekeek."

"And his uncle," Willy added.

LOST AND FOUND

The forest was a dangerous place back in the days of the early settlers. Bush farms were surrounded by trackless forest full of wild animals.

Travellers feared the lynx or wildcat.

Occasionally wanderers came across bears, but these could often be scared away by shouting.

Children were most likely to get lost while they were hunting for the family cow. Bessie was allowed to roam where she liked, but she had to be brought home every evening for milking. A child who put off fetching the cow could be caught by the dark.

A traveller who wandered away from the trail might fall into a swamp or break an ankle in a hole.

Knowing how to make a shelter and a fire could save your life. The Native people taught the pioneers how to build shelters like the one above. The shelters were then left on the trail for other travellers.

Early settlers carried small hatchets to cut wedge-shaped marks on trees along the trail. It was important to cut these patches at eye level and make them big enough to show white in the dark woods. Today, people often blaze trails with fluorescent paint.

People learned from experience — or were taught by the Native people — how to overcome the dangers. Native people signposted routes with marker trees. Branches of saplings would be tied into a shape that pointed out the direction. As the tree grew, the branch remained in the twisted shape and became a living signpost. A 200-year-old marker tree still stands on a trail in the Niagara peninsula.

Time to Play It Safe

Early settlers learned never to start into the woods close to evening. The sun might still be shining, but in the forest it would already be getting dark. Experienced woodsmen could often guess how long they had before sunset just by glancing at the sun's position. You can do it, too.

Stand in a place where you have a clear view of the sun above the horizon. Hold your arm out straight. Turn your hand in, keeping your fingers straight but your thumb tucked in. Position your hand so that it fits between the horizon and the bottom of the sun.

If you can fit four fingers between the horizon and the bottom of the sun, you have about one hour before sunset. If you can fit two fingers, you have roughly 30 minutes. If you have very small hands, you may need to use a watch to help you figure out how many of your fingers it takes to measure one hour.

MOVING DAY

A re we moving today?" Lizzie asked every morning at breakfast.
"Patience, patience. You want to have a bed to sleep in, don't you?"
Pa would say, or "We're waiting for the stove, lass. You don't want to
freeze now, do you? We'll be in before Christmas, I promise."

This went on for weeks while Pa and a hired man, with occasional
help from George and Willy, fitted windows and doors and finished off
scores of little jobs to make the house ready.

Sarah didn't mind the wait. She was making something special for
the new house, and she wanted it ready for the very day they moved in. She
had started by collecting different colours of yarn. Granny and Ma were
glad to give her leftover scraps, but Meg had the colour she really wanted.
"Just one strand, that's all I need," she begged Meg for what seemed like the
hundredth time, as they sat by the fire darning stockings one evening.

"Oh, all right, Miss Pest." Meg unwound the end of a ball of wool,
dyed dark red with her precious cochineal dye. It was all she had left after
the weaver had finished her coverlet, and she was being very careful how
she used it. She extended her arm and measured off a length from her
fingertips to her nose, just the way Mr. Jamieson at the general store
measured cloth. "That's all, mind you."

"Oh, thank you, Meg!" Sarah hadn't expected Meg to be so generous. She wrapped the rich red yarn neatly around two fingers, slipped it off and tucked it into her sewing basket. It was curled next to yarn dyed yellow from onion skins, a soft pink piece Granny had dyed from madder root, a blue one from her mother's indigo and a dark green from acorns.

Once Sarah had all the colours she needed, she stretched a piece of linen Ma had given her across a frame made of twigs. Then, every day before she went to school, she worked by the morning light, stitching a present for the new house.

"But what good is it?" Meg asked one day. She was deftly braiding shredded cornhusks to make a tough mat for the front door. "At least *this* will keep some of the mud out of the house."

"It will be pretty," Sarah stated firmly, but Meg's comment bothered her. Perhaps something useful would be better. Useful *and* pretty. The chair George was making, with its seat of woven hickory bark, would look elegant at the table and be comfortable to sit on. Willy, shaving a hickory branch to make a new broom, was certainly making something useful. Even Lizzie, poking bits of cloth through a piece of canvas to make a kitchen mat, was being practical.

"I don't care," Sarah decided, smoothing her hand over a spot where the linen wrinkled slightly under her tiny cross-stitching. "This is what I want to give the house." She had seen a stitched sampler hanging on Mrs. Burkholder's parlour wall. "That's how I practised sewing when I was your age," said Mrs. Burkholder. "When I finally made a good one, my mother put a frame around it and hung it on the wall."

As Pa finished the new house bit by bit, Sarah and Willy explored. They couldn't believe how big it was. They loved climbing up and down the stairs, hanging out the windows, imagining how their old furniture would fit in the new rooms. On the main floor was a kitchen with a built-in bake oven, a parlour and a bedroom. Upstairs was still one big open space. When Pa had time, he would divide it into bedrooms — one for the girls, one for the boys, one for Ma and Pa and one for company. Granny would sleep in the downstairs bedroom because the stairs were too much for her.

One day Sarah and Meg climbed the stairs to the second floor and planned their bedroom.

"We'll hang the looking-glass here," Meg decided, framing a spot on the wall with her hands. Now that she'd paid the weaver for her coverlet, Meg was saving up for a mirror she'd seen at the store.

Sarah had her own ideas. She had cut a stencil out of birch-bark so that she and Meg could paint a pattern around the edges of the floor. She was pleased that Meg approved of her pattern. Even if it is just pretty, Sarah thought stubbornly.

As November passed, Sarah too began to ask, "When are we going to move?" Now the answer was "Soon" and finally, "Very soon — before the end of the month."

I'll have to work faster, Sarah thought, as she sat stitching her sampler one morning. The thought made her prick her finger. She snatched it away just in time to prevent a drop of blood from falling on the creamy linen. It took a long time to set each stitch just right and make sure the lettering was straight. When the edging started to wobble, she had to pick out the stitches and start again. The day she finished the last stitch, a message came from Mr. Jamieson at the general store. Their parlour stove had been delivered at last!

"Tomorrow's moving day," Pa announced as he set off with the ox sled to fetch the stove.

The next morning, every hand was needed to move the family up the hill to the new house, so Willy and Sarah were allowed to stay home from school. While Pa and George struggled with stovepipes and Granny directed traffic, the rest packed wooden crates and barrels and kettles and baskets of things onto sleds and dragged them up the hill. Finally they had everything, even the big settle, in the new house.

George was carrying in wood to light the new stove when Sarah remembered her sampler. She had tucked it safely out of harm's way, but now it was time to fetch it.

She ran back down the hill, sliding on the tracks the sleds had made in the snow, and opened the door of the empty cabin. The fire had burned low, leaving a damp chill in the air. Sarah shivered, and a strange sadness swept over her. She'd never seen this room without a kettle of soup bubbling on the fire, Granny's spinning wheel in the corner, her own little stool pulled up to the fire. Empty, it looked forlorn and forsaken.

We're just moving up the hill, she reminded herself. Still, it was goodbye to the old life — crowded and dingy maybe, but also cosy and warm.

Just then Willy barged in and grabbed the broom he'd made. "Come on. We're ready to light the new stove."

Sarah's sadness vanished. She plucked her sampler from the mantel, where it lay protected by the goose-wing duster, and dashed up the hill after Willy.

Everyone was in the parlour. Meg lit the candles in the wall sconces. Granny twitched at the new rag rug, setting it just right in front of the day bed, and Willy set his new broom in the corner, even though it belonged in the kitchen.

"What a grand day for the Robertsons!" Ma said, as Pa touched the lighted splint to the kindling in the stove. "Our very first front parlour."

"And what better place for our very first clock," Pa said as he placed Ma's clock on the shelf he'd carved especially for it. "What have we here? A nail? I wonder what's to be hung on this nail?"

Sarah suddenly felt shy. Were they laughing at her? She felt her face go hot as she offered Pa the sampler. He held it up by the loop of yarn so that everyone could see.

Inside the border of slightly wobbly roses it said:

God Bless
our new house
And all who come within
The Robertson Family
November 1840

Ma put an arm around Sarah, and they stood together looking at the sampler. "The very thing we needed, Sarah — a blessing to make our new house a home."

"Aye, and years from now," Granny said, "when you're an old, old lady like me, you can point to that and tell your grandchildren about the day we moved into our fine new house."

THE SECOND HOUSE

Early settlers looked forward to building a large, comfortable house. When they first arrived in the backwoods, they had more important needs. They made do with a small cabin until they had cleared enough land to grow crops and had built a barn to store the grain and house their animals in the winter. Often it was ten years before they could turn their energies to building a comfortable house. The Robertsons' new house had all the "modern conveniences." Best of all, it had room to move around in. What a treat after the crowded little cabin!

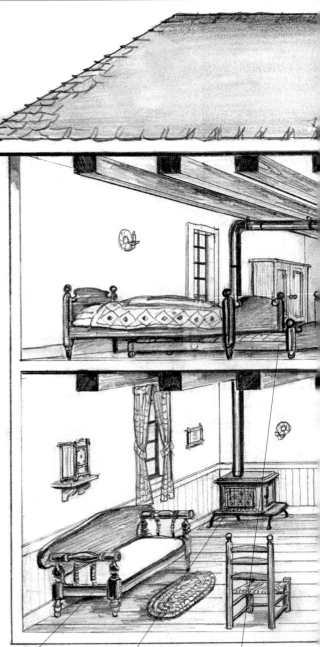

the cabin

the new house

The day bed was used for a nap after dinner time, before the men went back out to the fields, or by a sick child.

The box stove warmed the parlour, and pipes carried a little heat upstairs.

Beds were built high off the floor and often had a trundle-bed, for a child or for company, underneath.

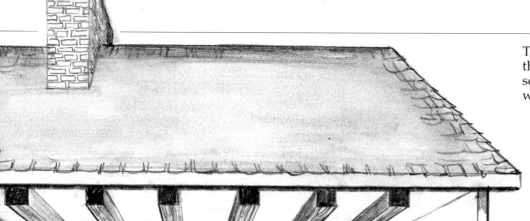

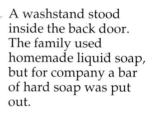

Tin sconces protected the wall from heat and soot when the candles were lit.

A washstand stood inside the back door. The family used homemade liquid soap, but for company a bar of hard soap was put out.

Ladder-back chairs with seats of woven hickory bark were a big improvement over benches and stump stools.

The dough box kept the bread dough warm while it was rising.

This indoor bake oven was a big improvement. Turn the page to find out why.

A bucket of water stood near the fireplace, in case of fire.

The dish dresser held tin or pewter plates and mugs, bowls hollowed from the burls of maple trees and a precious few crockery bowls.

The high-backed settle was often pulled close to the fire. The front opened to form a box that could be made into a bed for company or used as a playpen for the baby.

USING THE BAKE OVEN

With her large and growing family, Mrs. Robertson was glad to have an indoor bake oven so that she could bake several loaves of bread at once, summer or winter.

Bread making began in the evening. Mrs. Robertson often made potato bread. To half a pail of mashed potatoes she added four handfuls of flour, a handful of salt and two cupfuls of barm (yeast and water). She put this mixture in the dough box near the fire. Overnight, the dough doubled in size.

The next morning Mrs. Robertson punched down the dough, kneaded it and put it in a greased bowl to rise again.

Next she set a fire on the floor of the bake oven. Two hours later, when the risen dough filled the bowl, Mrs. Robertson put her hand into the oven to check on the temperature. Judging the temperature correctly meant the difference between well-baked bread and a rock-hard crust surrounding soggy dough.

When the oven temperature seemed to be right, Mrs. Robertson raked out the fire. Then, using a bread peel (a flat paddle with a long handle), she slid the round loaves into the oven. Last of all, she sealed the opening with a heavy wooden door to keep the heat in.

To time the baking, she made a mark on a candle. When the candle burned down to the mark, the bread would be ready. An experienced cook knew exactly how much candle marked an hour.

Mrs. Robertson made different kinds of bread depending on what supplies she had. White flour was hard to come by, so she saved it for special occasions or made it last longer by mixing in bran, cornmeal or potatoes. When she ran out of flour, she made corn bread in the bake kettle. Corn bread keeps longer than wheat bread, so it was often carried by travellers. This gave it the name "journey cake" or johnny cake.

Raising Bread

Bread dough is mostly flour and water. But if you baked this mixture, you'd get flat, hard biscuits. You need something to "leaven" the bread — make it light and tasty. That something is yeast.

Yeast is a fungus that lives on the sugar in plants. As it grows, it gives off a gas called carbon dioxide. When yeast is mixed into dough, the carbon dioxide gas is trapped in bubbles in the dough — and in the bread as it cooks. Yeast also adds that distinctive "bread" aroma and flavour.

Today you can buy packages of dried yeast. In the backwoods, settlers had to make their own by boiling the flowers of the hop vine. The resulting liquid, called barm, was kept in a stone crock, and two cupfuls were added to each batch of bread dough. If the settlers didn't have hop vines, they made "bread starter" by mixing a little salt and sugar into a cup of mashed potatoes and water. This was kept in a warm place to ferment or bubble up. Every time a cupful was used, the starter was topped up with a mixture of flour and potato water.

Homemade yeast didn't always work. Farm families ate a lot of hard or soggy bread. Anyone who could bake a light, fluffy loaf every time was celebrated throughout the community.

Stencilling

When the Robertsons had time, they painted their new house inside and out with homemade paint made by mixing skim milk with lime, linseed oil and powdered colours such as brick red or yellow. Mrs. Robertson and the girls used a stencil to paint a border around the parlour walls. They even stencilled a pattern all over the floor to look like a carpet. You can use stencil designs to make wrapping paper or book covers.

You'll need:
- tracing paper
- a pencil
- carbon paper
- a square of cardboard or stiff paper 8 cm x 8 cm (3 inches x 3 inches)
- utility knife
- a sheet of paper to stencil on
- thick tempera paint (or marking pens or crayons)
- paintbrush

1. Use the tracing paper to trace one of the pioneer designs below or draw your own.

2. Put the carbon paper, shiny side down, over the cardboard square. Put the tracing paper on top and trace over the design with a pencil. Press heavily so the design will transfer onto your square.

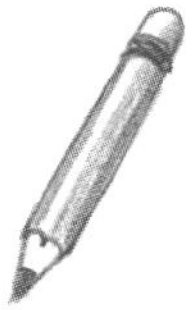

3. Ask an adult to help you use the utility knife to cut out the design. Be careful not to cut through the thin parts that separate the sections of the design. When you are done, your stencil is ready to use.

4. Spread the paper you are going to decorate on the table. Starting at one corner, lay the stencil on the sheet. Paint over the design with a brush. If you are using marking pens or crayons, colour in the design. Hold the stencil down firmly and work from the outside of the stencil in.

5. When the design has been filled in, lift the stencil straight up so that you don't smudge the paint.

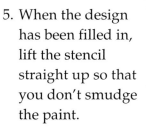

6. Position the stencil where you want the next design to appear. Be careful not to put the stencil back down on the newly painted design. Continue stencilling until you are satisfied with the look.

7. Experiment with ways of putting the colour on. Small sponge pads or pads of cheesecloth give an interesting effect. Once you have mastered the technique, try stencilling cardboard or wooden boxes.

BUILDING BEDS

In the log cabin, the girls and Mr. and Mrs. Robertson had slept on wood-framed bunks built right into the walls. Saplings were fitted crosswise into the frames to hold the mattresses. Before the family could move into the new house, Mr. Robertson had to build new beds.

The new beds had wooden frames with rope laced across them to act as springs. Often the rope stretched, making the springs sag. To make the bed comfortable again, the rope was tightened by turning the peg at the side of the bed. On beds with no turn peg, a child walked around on the springs, shifting the rope until the sag was "walked out."

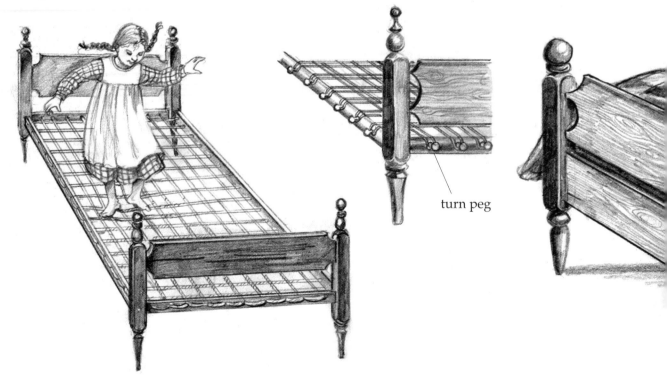

turn peg

Over the rope were laid one or two ticks — linen bags filled with straw or shredded cornhusks. The straw bunched up at night, so in the morning the bed-maker had to even out the straw and make the bed smooth. As the straw dried out, it broke into small sharp bits that poked through the covering. Sarah loved it when they took the ticks out to the field, dumped out the old, dusty, broken bits and filled each tick with new, sweet straw.

In time, to make the beds warmer and softer, Mrs. Robertson made feather mattresses to go over the ticks. Linen sheets and quilts finished the beds. Mrs. Robertson and Meg and Granny spent many of their evenings piecing together bits of fabric to make quilts for the whole family.

CHRISTMAS VISITING

The barking of a dog woke Sarah from her half-doze. She sat up in the sled, and the sudden movement made her head pound. Where was that hanky? She blew her nose. Lizzie stretched and yawned beside her.

"Are we there, Granny?" Lizzie popped out from under the buffalo robe, letting cold air flood in.

"Careful, careful." Granny shifted a sleeping Tommy to her other arm and rearranged the covering. Tucked warmly into a straw nest covered with a buffalo robe, the four of them were on the box sled that Pa and George were pulling through the snowy forest to the Burkholders'. Ma and Meg and Willy walked behind.

Sarah hunted in the covers for her second handkerchief. She'd been allowed to ride on the sled because she'd been sick with a bad cold. "Stay bundled up," Ma had said, tucking her in. "And here's something to help that stuffy nose." The scrap of linen dipped in camphor had disappeared into the covers while Sarah slept. Just as she found it, they came out of the trees into the Burkholders' farmyard. The dog's yipping roused the house. The door flew open, flooding the front porch with light.

"Here at last!" Uncle Jacob boomed out. "Welcome, welcome." Arms lifted Tommy and Lizzie from the sled. Sarah crawled, shivering, over the tongue and stood looking in the door. Christmas Eve was special in the Burkholder household. How clearly she remembered from last year the smell of spice cookies, the warmth and gaiety and, best of all — the tree. Would they have one again this year?

"Come in, my friends. Come in." Soon they were in the kitchen, rubbing the chill from their hands in front of the fire and talking a mile a minute.

"How kind of you to invite us, Nettie." Ma offered Mrs. Burkholder a crock full of oatcakes and shortbreads.

"How nice of you to come, Janet." Aunt Nettie set the crock on a table already covered with plates of cookies and candies.

What funny things they say, grown-ups, thought Sarah. She pressed the hanky under her nose to keep from sneezing, while her eyes searched the room. No tree. Maybe it's in the parlour.

The room seemed full of strangers. A young man and woman shook hands with Pa. They must be Uncle Jacob's son and his wife, from the other side of the river. Three children sat wide-eyed and silent on a bench by the fire. Lizzie edged over to stare eyeball to eyeball with the eldest, a boy who looked about her own age.

Sarah was too far from the parlour to sneak a quick look through the doorway. Everyone was sitting down now, Meg with her interminable knitting, Pa bouncing Tommy on his knee so he wouldn't want to crawl around. Perhaps they don't have one this year, Sarah thought. She blinked back tears.

"I know what the children want," Aunt Nettie said. "Before we settle down, let's just go and look."

Sarah's heart leaped. She went hot and cold with excitement as she followed Aunt Nettie into the parlour. And there it was! Just as beautiful as last year. A fir tree, nearly reaching the ceiling, set up in the corner. Festoons of popcorn and cranberries swirled around it, gingerbread cookies hung by threads, balls of dyed fleece dotted its branches. Sarah looked again. Yes, there they were — tiny candles that Aunt Nettie had made especially for Christmas, clipped to every branch.

Aunt Nettie lifted the lid of the box stove and lit a splint. "Here, Sarah," she said. "You light them this year."

Hands shaking, Sarah took the splint.

"Let me help," Ma said, holding Sarah's arm steady.

"Yeah," George muttered. "Don't wanna burn us out."

But even George couldn't spoil this moment. Not daring to breathe for fear of extinguishing the tiny flame, Sarah reached out and touched each wick. As the last one glowed into life, the murmurs and sighs told her how beautiful it was. She stepped back to look, and the sight brought a glaze of tears that made the tiny lights blur and grow bigger until the whole tree shone.

"Oh, how I wish *we* could have a tree like this," she breathed. "How I wish …"

CHRISTMAS IN THE BACKWOODS

The Burkholders were German settlers from Pennsylvania and had brought with them the German custom of decorating an evergreen tree for Christmas. The tiny candles were lit for only a few minutes at a time because of the danger of fire. On Christmas Eve, a neighbour often dressed up in a mask as Belsnickel and visited households, bringing candies for good children and a switch to frighten bad children. On Christmas morning, the children hoped to find candies shaped like animals waiting on their plates.

As Christmas approached, English settlers bought raisins and spices at the general store so they could make mince pies and plum pudding. They dragged a huge oak log in and kept it burning for the Twelve Days of Christmas. This yule-log custom goes back to early pagan times. English settlers fattened several geese through the fall to be ready for Christmas dinner. Children looked forward to presents of oranges (precious because they could be bought only at this time of year) and candies. Gifts weren't exchanged, but Mother might knit new mittens or hats for the younger ones, and Father might carve a toy for the baby.

Irish settlers had their own customs. On Christmas Eve the youngest child placed a lit candle in the window to welcome Mary and Joseph. The Mary of the family — almost every family had a Mary — snuffed out the candle on Christmas Day. Irish families also made small nativity scenes to help the children understand the Christmas story.

Santa Claus came to North America with Dutch settlers, who first called him Saint Nicholas, then Sinter Klaas and finally Santa Claus.

The Robertsons were surprised to find their neighbours celebrating Christmas. In Scotland, it was a day to spend quietly in church. Their festive day was New Year's Eve.

As the years passed, settlers in the backwoods and in the towns borrowed ideas from their neighbours and soon, instead of a German or Irish or English Christmas, there was a distinctly North American Christmas.

Saint Nicholas

Candle Dipping

Pioneer families made tallow candles for everyday use. For special occasions, they often made a few candles from beeswax or the waxy, aromatic coating of bayberries imported from the Atlantic provinces. Ask an adult to help you make dipped candles for your own special occasion. (Warning: Paraffin wax catches fire easily if it gets too hot. Drips of hot wax can burn your skin.)

You'll need:
- newspapers
- a metre stick or broom handle propped between two chairs
- water
- a large pot
- 2 sticks of paraffin wax
- an empty 1.36-L (48-ounce) can with one end removed
- scissors
- 60 cm (24 inches) of candlewick

1. Put old newspapers under the broom handle. You will be hanging the dripping candles here while they harden.

2. Pour water into the pot to a depth of 5 cm (2 inches). Ask an adult to turn the burner on low and heat the water.

3. Place the paraffin wax in the can and place the can in the water in the pot. The paraffin will slowly melt.

4. Cut the candlewick into 20-cm (8-inch) lengths.

5. When the wax has melted, ask an adult to help you lower half of one candlewick into the wax. Slowly lift it out and hold it until the wax begins to cool and harden. Then lower the wick again so more wax will coat it. Lift it and let it cool again. Repeat this until the candle is the thickness you want.

6. Tie the wick onto the broom handle and leave the candle to cool. After several hours, when the candle has hardened, cut the wick off 1 cm ($\frac{1}{2}$ inch) above the wax. Store the candle in a cool place until you need it.

7. Repeat for all the lengths of candlewick. Add more paraffin if necessary. Pour the leftover paraffin into a dish to harden and keep for your next candle-making session.

WINTER TRAVEL

Winter was a season for festivity. All the hard work of producing food was over. As a result, families had more time for visiting.

Travelling was easier, too. Roads that were muddy quagmires in rainy weather or rutted and uneven in dry weather were frozen hard and paved smooth with a thick coating of snow in the winter. It was a good time for the family to visit far-away relatives or for young people to drive into town to a ball.

The Robertsons couldn't afford a horse and cutter just yet. They used their oxen to pull the big sleigh, or they pulled a smaller sled themselves. The Burkholders, who had been established for much longer, did have a horse and cutter. Cutters with iron runners could move quickly over a snow-packed road. To prevent collisions, drivers strung bells along the horses' harnesses. This merry jingling warned other drivers that a sleigh was near. "Keep to your right" was the rule of the road for sleighs then, just as it is for cars now. Even so, many a sleighful of party-goers was flung into a snowdrift when drivers got to racing or a sudden noise startled the horses.

the Robertsons' big sleigh

the Burkholders' cutter

ROADS

In the early days, the way a person travelled depended on two circumstances: the state of the road and the state of his purse. Many settlers were forced to use what they called "shank's mare" — their own two feet — to get from place to place. Those who could afford wagons, sleighs or carriages had to worry about the condition of the roads.

As an area was opened for settlement, surveyors marked out roadways. Axemen followed, chopping down trees, which were cleared away by road gangs with teams of oxen.

Although these workmen opened wide swaths through the forest, they didn't smooth the road surface. For years, travellers had to navigate around stumps and ruts. In spring and fall the roads were impassable mud holes, in summer dust-choked nightmares.

At first, footpaths and portage trails were the only routes through the woods.

Working on the roads was a settlement duty. A farm had to provide one man and two oxen for four days of work each year. The farmer appointed to be "road boss" rounded up his crew and tackled the local roads.

Men and oxen pulled out stumps, ploughed the surface smooth, laid cedar logs side by side across swampy areas or built low-level log bridges across streams.

These log roads and bridges, called corduroy roads, made for bumpy driving. The dirt and gravel that filled the gaps between the logs quickly washed out, leaving holes big enough to trap a horse's hoof or to jolt off a wagon wheel. In rainy weather the logs were often afloat on a river of mud.

Over the years the roads were gradually smoothed, good gravel beds were laid, and farmers could drive their wagons to market in any weather. But in the early years, people lucky enough to live by a lake or a deep river used canoes, bateaux or steamers for much of their travelling.

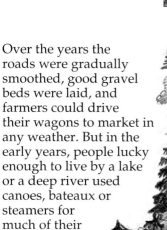

HOGMANAY

Rise up, guidwife, and shake your feathers!
Dinna think that we are beggars,
We're girls and boys come out today
For to get our Hogmanay!

Willy strode up to the door and knocked sharply as the chorus of young voices behind him chanted "Rise up, good wife …"

Granny opened the door. "What's this? What's this? Beggars come with their hands out?"

"It's us, Granny. It's us!" Lizzie screeched, jumping up and down until the new porch floor squeaked.

"Och, just so." Granny's eyes teased them. "And what would you be wanting, now?"

"Say it," Sarah urged her little sister.

"Girls and boys come out today …"

"For to get our Hogmanay," Sarah finished.

"Here you are then." Granny tumbled tiny oatcakes into the cupped hands, six each. The cakes were sweetened with honey Ma had saved just for these special New Year's Eve cakes. The children trooped into the house with their treasure.

Not quite as much fun as the way Granny described Hogmanay in Scotland, Sarah thought, remembering Granny's stories about knocking on all the doors in the village on New Year's Eve and coming home with a whole apronful of oatcakes. But then, where would you find other doors out here in the middle of nowhere?

"Time we were getting things ready," Ma said. "Sarah, grind some spices for the ale. Meg, put out the wee cakes and the shortbread."

The house had smelled wonderful for a week with all the baking. "Don't you touch one crumb," Ma had warned them. Not long now, Sarah thought, her mouth watering.

Granny was crotchety. "Where's my broom gone, then?"

"Here, Gran," Meg said. "I was just sweeping snow off the steps."

"You leave it be. I want it right to hand. I intend to give the old year a good sweep out that back door at midnight. We want all to go well with this new house."

Meg rolled her eyes as her grandmother snatched the broom and thumped it down beside the back door. But Sarah, grinding away at the spices, smiled secretly. She liked the idea of sweeping the old year out. In the cabin they'd had no back door — no way to get rid of the old year.

"What's that?" Willy looked up from the hearth, where he was nibbling an oatcake. "Sleigh bells?"

"Ah, they're here," Pa said, coming in from the parlour. "George, run and see to the horse." As George opened the front door, Sarah heard the sound of boots crunching over snow and stamping up the steps. Uncle Jacob Burkholder stood on the door sill.

"Good health and happiness to this house and all in it," he boomed. His voice, Sarah was sure, filled every nook and cranny. "And may none but friends cross this threshold."

"Get along, Jacob, get along," Aunt Nettie scolded from behind. "You're letting the cold air in. Now where's Lizzie? Look what I have for you, *Liebchen.*"

Lizzie came running, hands out, for the carved wooden doll dressed in a scrap of brown linen. Aunt Nettie had a small gift for every child, a Jacob's ladder for Willy, a top for Tommy, a game of noughts and crosses for Sarah, all carved by Uncle Jacob's clever jackknife.

The evening settled down to talking and storytelling with delicious intervals of nibbling. Sarah was yawning and Lizzie was fast asleep on the settle when George said, "It's quarter to midnight."

"Help me up, Sarah," Granny said. "I need to get my broom." Sarah held out her hands and braced her feet as her grandmother pulled herself out of the rocker and hobbled over to the door.

"But who will be the first-footer?" Willy wanted to know. "How can we have good luck in the new house without a first-footer?"

"Someone will show up," his mother assured him.

Sarah caught the wink Ma and Pa exchanged. She intended to watch carefully for the moment when Pa sneaked out.

"Are you sure that clock is right, Janet?"

"Of course it is." Ma didn't like to be teased, not even by Uncle Jacob. "I've tested it against the sun any number of times. It's never been wrong yet."

"Are you ready, then?" Granny wanted all their attention on the back door. "Open it up, Willy, my wee man!"

Cold air swirled in, brightening the fire. Everyone crowded around to watch Granny. From the hearth, across the new floor to the sill, she swept and swept until Sarah thought she could almost see the old year flying out the door into the winter night.

Everyone cheered and clapped.

"One minute to go," Willy shouted, slamming the back door shut.

Sarah fixed her eyes on Pa. He put his mug of cider down on the table, exchanging a glance and a nod with Ma. But before he could move, there came a thunderous knocking on the front door. Sarah's heart jumped. Even Ma looked startled. "Who's there?" she exclaimed.

"First-footer!" Willy shrieked and ran to throw open the door. A tall, black-haired man stood on the porch.

"Good health to this house and all in it!" he cried, holding out a small round loaf of bread. Sarah couldn't see what was in his other hand.

"Och, now, isn't that the luck," crowed Granny. "Come in, come in. And what's this you're bringing? Food for the coming year? A proper first-footer you are for the new house!"

A laughing Pa pulled the young man into the house. It was Uncle Jacob's son.

"Here's your bread, ma'am," he said to Ma, "and here," he added, tipping glowing embers from a cedar cone into the already roaring fire, "here's your warmth and comfort for the coming year."

"Well now," Pa said, and this time his wink was for Sarah, "didn't we promise someone would turn up?"

NEW YEAR'S CELEBRATIONS

The Robertsons' festive day was New Year's Eve, which the Scottish call Hogmanay. Mrs. Robertson started preparing several days ahead of time with a thorough cleaning of the house (no one wants to go dirty into the new year!) and special baking with the butter and white flour she saved for this occasion.

The Robertson children followed the Scottish custom of begging for treats. There were many different verses that could be sung to bring someone to the door with handouts of sweetened oatcakes:

Hogmanay, troll-ol, troll-aye,
Give of your white bread and none of your grey.
My feet are cold, my shoes are thin,
Give me cakes and let me in.

Later in the evening, friends gathered to celebrate with spiced ale, shortbread, oatcakes and blackbun, a festive cake made with raisins and spices and baked in a pastry covering. To ensure luck for the coming year, the oldest person sliced the blackbun, and the youngest carried it around to everyone in the room.

At midnight, the back door was opened to let the old year out, and the front door was opened to let the new year in. If the first visitor of the new year was a dark-haired man carrying ale, salt or bread and coal (representing food and warmth), the family would surely have good luck all year. Sometimes they helped the luck along by sending out a "first-footer," as he was called, just before midnight, so that the right kind of visitor would be first across the threshold.

Jumping Jack

Wooden toys whittled in the evening around the fire were among the few playthings in pioneer homes. Spinning tops, climbing bears, a set of clatter blocks called Jacob's ladder and jumping jacks were the most popular. Make your own jumping jack.

You'll need:
- tracing paper
- a pencil
- scissors
- sticky tape
- heavy cardboard
- markers or crayons
- a nail or skewer
- 6 brass paper fasteners
- string

1. Draw the body parts you see at the top of the next page on the cardboard. Yours can be much bigger than the ones shown, but try to draw similar shapes. Cut out the cardboard pieces.

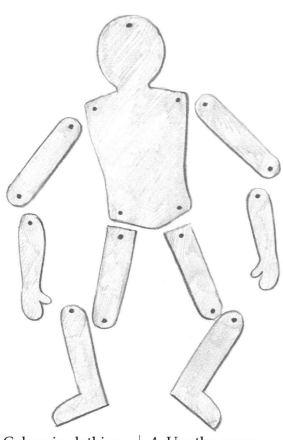

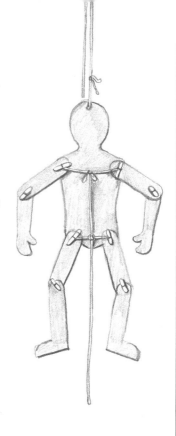

5. Cut one piece of string long enough to make a loop. Thread it through the top of the head and knot it.

6. Cut two more pieces of string. Tie one to the fasteners at the shoulders. Tie the second piece to the fasteners at the hips.

7. Tie another piece of string to the shoulder and hip strings. Let the tail of the string hang free.

2. Colour in clothing and a face.

3. Use a nail or skewer to punch holes in the places shown by the black dots.

4. Use the paper fasteners to fasten the arms and legs to the body.

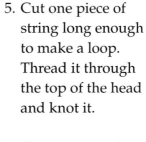

8. To work the jumping jack, hold it by the loop on the head and pull the hanging string. The arms and legs will jump and flex.

GLOSSARY

backwoods — heavily wooded or partly cleared areas far from towns

bake oven — a brick oven, sometimes built into one side of the fireplace, sometimes a separate structure built outdoors. The bake oven was used for baking bread and pastries.

bait — a lure, usually food, used to attract fish or animals in order to catch them

camphor — a strong-smelling liquid made from the wood of the laurel tree and sniffed to help clear clogged sinuses

cauldron — a very large iron pot (sometimes more than a metre [yard] in diameter) with a hooped handle, used for boiling

churn — a container in which cream is beaten or shaken to form butter

crock — an earthenware jar produced in many sizes

crossbeam — a beam or large squared support timber fastened between two walls

ember — a small, glowing-hot piece of wood from a fire

fleece — the coat of wool covering a sheep

grizzle — the soft mewling (whining) sound made by a hungry or uncomfortable baby (Scottish dialect)

hearth — the stone or brick floor of a fireplace. The hearth extended into the room to protect the wooden floors from sparks.

husk — the dry outer covering of certain seeds; the outer covering of an ear of corn.

kettle — an iron pot with a hooped handle, used for boiling. A kettle is smaller than a cauldron.

kindling — small, dry, splintery pieces of wood used for starting a fire

pioneer — a person who does something first and so prepares the way for others; a person who settles in a region that has not been settled before.

resin — a sticky, gummy substance that oozes from pine and fir trees. Resin can be used to waterproof canoes or to make wood flammable.

settle — a long wooden bench with arms and a high back. A settle was often used as a spare bed.

settler — a person who comes to live in a newly cleared farming area

shanty — a small, roughly built hut, which was often the settler's first shelter

stoneboat — a small sled with no runners used for sliding stones and other heavy objects over short distances

stook — ten to twelve wheat sheaves standing on end and leaning on one another. Stooking wheat in the field speeds up the drying process.

tick — a cloth covering stuffed with straw or corn husks and used as a mattress

tinder — anything that catches fire easily, usually dried moss, rotted wood (punk) or charred linen. Tinder was used to catch sparks to start a fire.

underbrush — bushes and small trees growing under large trees in a wood or forest

windrow — a row of hay or grain raked up in the field to dry before being hauled to the barn for storage

ANSWER

Hen-house Mystery, page 54

A few tell-tale feathers and tracks heading away from the hen house told Mr. Robertson that during the night a fox had sneaked in and stolen one of the chickens.

INDEX